THE

Best American Novels
OF THE Twentieth Century

Still Readable Today

Eleanor M. Gehres

Fulcrum Publishing
Golden, Colorado

Library of Congress Cataloging-in-Publication Data
Gehres, Eleanor M.
  The best American novels of the twentieth century still readable today / Eleanor Agnew Mount Gehres.
    p. cm.
  ISBN 1-55591-453-5
  1. American fiction—20th century—Bibliography. 2. Best books—United States. I. Title.
  Z1231.F4 G36 2001
  [PS379]
  015.73′073—dc21
                                                      2001003073

Printed in the United States of America

0 9 8 7 6 5 4 3 2 1

Editorial: Robert C. Baron, Lori D. Kranz, Lesley Juel, Katharine Baron
Jacket and interior design: Patty Maher
Cover image: Photogear Skyscapes from Image Club

Fulcrum Publishing
16100 Table Mountain Parkway, Suite 300
Golden, Colorado 80403
(800) 992-2908 • (303) 277-1623
www.fulcrum-books.com

Contents

35	Douglas, Lloyd C.	*The Robe*	1942
10	Dreiser, Theodore	*An American Tragedy*	1925
54	Drury, Allen	*Advise and Consent*	1959
22	Edmonds, Walter D.	*Drums Along the Mohawk*	1936
54	Ellison, Ralph	*Invisible Man*	1952
23	Farrell, James T.	*Studs Lonigan: A Trilogy*	1935
14	Faulkner, William	*The Sound and the Fury*	1929
11	Ferber, Edna	*So Big*	1924
70	Fisher, Vardis	*Mountain Man*	1965
11	Fitzgerald, F. Scott	*The Great Gatsby*	1925
108	Frazier, Charles	*Cold Mountain*	1997
90	Gardner, John	*Nickel Mountain*	1973
23	Glasgow, Ellen	*Vein of Iron*	1935
6	Grey, Zane	*Riders of the Purple Sage*	1912
71	Green, Hannah	*I Never Promised You a Rose Garden*	1964
109	Guterson, David	*Snow Falling on Cedars*	1994
36	Guthrie, Jr., A. B.	*The Big Sky*	1947
24	Hammett, Dashiell	*The Maltese Falcon*	1930
71	Heinlein, Robert A.	*Stranger in a Strange Land*	1961
72	Heller, Joseph	*Catch-22*	1961
36	Hemingway, Ernest	*For Whom the Bell Tolls*	1940
37	Hersey, John	*A Bell for Adano*	1944
25	Hilton, James	*Lost Horizon*	1933
38	Hobson, Laura Z.	*Gentleman's Agreement*	1947
38	Hodgins, Eric	*Mr. Blandings Builds His Dream House*	1946
55	Hunter, Evan	*The Blackboard Jungle*	1954
56	Hyman, Mac	*No Time for Sergeants*	1954
91	Irving, John	*The World According to Garp*	1978
12	James, Will	*Smoky, the Cowhorse*	1926
57	Jones, James	*From Here to Eternity*	1951
58	Kantor, MacKinlay	*Andersonville*	1955
73	Kaufman, Bel	*Up the Down Staircase*	1965
99	Kennedy, William	*Ironweed*	1983
59	Kerouac, Jack	*On the Road*	1957
74	Kesey, Ken	*One Flew over the Cuckoo's Nest*	1962
110	Kingsolver, Barbara	*Pigs in Heaven*	1993
59	Knowles, John	*A Separate Peace*	1959
91	Kosinski, Jerzy	*Being There*	1971
6	Lardner, Ring	*You Know Me Al*	1916
74	Lee, Harper	*To Kill a Mockingbird*	1960
12	Lewis, Sinclair	*Babbitt*	1922

Publisher's Preface

In September 1994, as part of the celebration of the forthcoming millennium, I asked Eleanor Gehres to write a book, *What America Was Reading*, a list of the one hundred best American books: novels, plays, poetry, history, biographies, and other nonfiction of the twentieth century. Eleanor, being herself, quickly decided that her book should include only fiction. Then she decided that she could not recommend any book unless she read it anew. If she had read it during her college days or even a few years ago, it had to be reread. For the next five years, Eleanor took book after book home to read. The list of "best" books grew to 150. She must have looked at many times that number.

The title was changed to *The Best American Novels of the Twentieth Century Still Readable Today*. Eleanor described her project: "Books that every educated person should read, books of inspiration, literary classics—wait, how about good books to enjoy on a cold winter's night or on a vacation? One hundred fifty American novels that may have been popular or won awards but more importantly are a pleasure to read today. Rediscover old friends or explore new worlds."

As her cancer grew, Eleanor slowed down but continued to work on her book. She was still reading and making notes when she died on March 18, 2000. At the time of her death, Eleanor could have taught a course on American literature at any university in the country. When her papers were sorted, her husband, Jim, and I found a list of one hundred and fifty books, reviews on one hundred and twenty five of them, and notes on several others. We decided to finish the book. Her friends read anew and wrote reviews of the remaining books.

The Best American Novels of the Twentieth Century is organized as Eleanor planned. Each decade begins with a list of events, followed by the chosen books in alphabetical order of authors' names. This provides a framework to understand the world that the author was witnessing and allows the reader to compare contemporary books and authors. On pages 114–119 you'll find a list of all selected books to enable you to keep a life list of books read.

Twenty-nine of these books won the Pulitzer Prize for fiction. Seven of the authors won the Nobel Prize for literature. Yet this is more than a list of award-winning books. Eleanor did not always follow popularity. She selected *Vein of Iron* rather than *In This Our Life* which won the Pulitzer for Ellen Glascow and A. B. Guthrie's *The Big Sky* rather than *The Way West*. In every case, Eleanor was looking for a "good read."

This book is being published in a limited edition of twelve hundred copies for presentation to Eleanor's friends and family, for her fellow librarians, and for people interested in western history and the world of books. For some people, like some books, live on in the memories of others.

Eleanor Agnew Mount Gehres was born in Riverside, New Jersey, February 18, 1932, and graduated from Mary Washington College at the University of Virginia with a degree in English literature in 1952. She began work as a schoolteacher in Norfolk, Virginia and then in Colorado Springs, where she met and married Edwin James "Jim" Gehres in 1960. The couple moved to Denver in 1961 and she worked as a teacher and librarian at Garden Place Elementary School in Globeville. After receiving her masters degree's in history and library science from the University of Denver, Eleanor went to work in the Denver Public Library's Western History Department in 1969 and became its manager in 1974. Eleanor's long list of awards includes the Lifetime Achievement Award from the Colorado Library Association and the Wallace Stegner Award from Colorado University's Center of the American West.

As *The Denver Post* said in its editorial of March 25, 2000: "Eleanor Gehres was never the kind of librarian who said 'Shhh.' In the 25 years she reigned over the Western History and Genealogy Department of the Denver Public Library, she set new standards both for the welcome extended to library clients and for the wonders of the collection that awaited them inside her bustling domain.

Librarians are very special people. They are caregivers of the world of the mind, the nurturers of dreams and the defenders of truth. Perhaps no other profession is so marked by the singular generosity of its practitioners."

And so this book is dedicated to Eleanor Gehres and to the special people who are librarians in America.

—*Robert C. Baron*

The 1900s
The New Century

A hurricane hits Galveston, Texas; thousands die.

Hershey opens a chocolate factory.

Earthquake and fires demolish San Francisco.

Ford produces the new Model T—"a motorcar for the multitudes."

The Wright brothers fly a heavier-than-air machine.

Einstein creates the theory of relativity, $e = mc^2$.

President William McKinley is assassinated.

The New York City subway opens to the public.

Theodore Roosevelt proposes conservation of public lands.

Barnum's Animal Crackers are introduced by the National Biscuit Company.

At the St. Louis World's Fair the ice-cream cone is created in a stall selling waffles.

Construction of the Panama Canal begins. It opens in 1914.

The Call of the Wild
Jack London (1876–1916)
New York: Macmillan, 1903

Here is an exciting adventure story of the travails of a civilized dog in the time of the Alaska gold rush. Buck, king of Judge Miller's place in Santa Clara, is shanghaied to the Northland, beaten by a dog broker, and repeatedly sold. In order to survive he must revert to the primordial but proud beast, using cunning and intelligence and drawing on instincts of his breed from prehistoric times. His struggles against all odds are as appealing today as when the story was first serialized in the *Saturday Evening Post* in 1900 and published as a book in 1903.

Jack London, an American realist writer, presents images of clash and struggle that align his stories with the American culture of the day

1

and Theodore Roosevelt's praise of the strenuous life. In time these instincts become irresistible impulses, the call of the wild.

London writes from his own experiences, and Buck is modeled on the dog that he befriended in the Yukon. Like Buck, London had been uprooted from California to the wilderness and learned to survive. In its time the novel was an instant best-seller, critically acclaimed, and made the author's name well known. It is still read in high school English classes and is deserving of a broader following.

The Circular Staircase
Mary Roberts Rinehart (1876–1958)
Indianapolis: Bobbs Merrill, 1908

A large rented summerhouse with mysterious rooms and stairways, things that go bump in the night, and an inability to retain hired staff are precursors of evil to come. The proper Miss Innes with her maid, Liddy, is a stalwart woman who will not be driven away to the city. All will be well with the arrival of her niece and nephew until a murder occurs and Miss Innes becomes a detective to protect her own kin. Told in the first person, the murder mystery retains its ability to tease and torment, as the solution is reached.

Mary Roberts Rinehart was a prolific writer of American fiction and was often favorably compared to her British contemporary, Agatha Christie. Some of the techniques, such as the asking of "why do you suppose?" type questions and commenting on incidents that would have future implications, date the mystery genre but do not negatively affect the story. Well-written and still a well-plotted, timeless adventure mystery.

The Jungle
Upton Sinclair (1878–1968)
New York: Doubleday, 1906

Written at times in a somewhat stilted journalistic style, Sinclair's book tells the story of Lithuanian refugees, Jurgis and Ona and their extended family, coming to the Promised Land of Packingtown in Chicago. Because of their naiveté, lack of English skills, and the bewildering chaos of urban life, they are constantly taken advantage of by shop-keepers, real estate agents, political hacks, and, most tragically, their employers in the huge meatpacking houses. As a result they subsist in dire poverty in spite of their diligence, and their existence is desperate due to backbreaking labor at slave wages. They work in abominable conditions and are expendable if taken ill or injured. With no money for medical attention, death is always a threat. Jurgis will get other tem-porary jobs with the manufacturers of tractors and the steel mills, but his fate and that of his family do not change. They sink deeper into poverty where the only escape is to die. Eventually Jurgis runs away to the nomadic life of a tramp.

This is a shocking book that tried to change the world and can be read to understand the power of the written word. Although the characters tend to be one-dimensional, the novel is still interesting and readable, if not at the top of the reading list. Sinclair, a somewhat successful cham-pion of political reform, tells his tale in unflinching detail and is an expert storyteller. His character Jurgis must undergo an inordinate amount of events if Sinclair is to reveal all the economic, social, and political ills of Chicago as a microcosm of the United States.

A Girl of the Limberlost
Gene Stratton Porter (1863–1924)
New York: Grosset & Dunlap, 1909

With its pedantic language, a heroine too good to be true, surrounded by well-meaning and sometimes misguided adults, *Girl* can still be read as a period piece. The taunting by teenagers of anyone who is different does not change with the ages. Characters around Elnora change over-night from bad people to good people when they realize the error of their ways.

Although the morals and customs of the times used to propel the plot are dated, the story itself holds one's interest. Anyone fascinated by natu-ral history, especially by plants grown in the swamps of the Limberlost (Indiana) or by the moths collected there, will find the book fulfilling. Will Philip Ammon win his Elnora and reject the superficial Edith Carr? Will Mrs. Comstock learn her husband's horrible secret and accept her rejected daughter? Will Elnora earn the money for college? The reader will not care as much as one should, given what appears today as artificial tragedies, but times have changed and even readers can change from naysayers to supporters. It's worth reading.

The Virginian
Owen Wister (1860–1938)
New York: Macmillan, 1902

It's hard to believe anyone would try to write a Western after *The Virginian* was published, but many have with varying results. As the book approaches its one hundredth anniversary, it is still one of the best (if not *the* best) of its genre. Its strengths lie in seeing a believable Wyoming ranching world through eastern eyes and its strong characters (so many times duplicated they now must overcome stereotypes).

Here are the tenderfoot; the strong silent handsome cowboy; and the pretty but independent eastern bred schoolmarm. Only the Virginian in 1901 could say with a straight face, "When you call me that, *smile.*" The adventures and misadventures on Judge Henry's Sunk Creek Ranch and in the surrounding countryside reflect the hardship of the times. Usually intelligence and tact are used by the foreman—the Virginian—in handling mutiny and other serious problems and he reaches for the gun or fists only in emergencies. Humor is at first the more effective weapon between the Virginian and Trampas, the man who hates him. Thus, violence to enforce the law is an unexpected climax to the story.

The love story as the cowboy woos the schoolmarm is classic. In spite of being diluted by its often poor imitators, *The Virginian* is still a Western at its finest with memorable characters set against a spectacular background. A plus: read a copy illustrated by Charles Russell.

The 1910s
Progressive Ideals and World War I

The Federal banking system and Federal Reserve Act are established.

Income Tax is authorized by a constitutional amendment.

General Pershing invades Mexico, chasing Pancho Villa.

Jeanette Rankin, of Montana, is the first woman elected to Congress.

The tango is the dance craze, but is banned in Boston.

The "unsinkable" *Titanic* sinks.

Mack Sennett's Keystone Kops make the country laugh.

The Eighteenth Amendment makes alcohol illegal, initializing prohibition.

The passenger pigeon becomes extinct.

F. W. Woolworth "Five and Dimes" are the largest retail chain in the world.

Jim Thorpe wins gold medals at the Olympic Games.

The influenza epidemic of 1918 claims millions of lives.

Winesburg, Ohio
Sherwood Anderson (1876–1941)
New York: B. W. Huebsch, 1919

This is a collection of twenty-three stories about the people who reside in a small midwestern town as seen through the eyes of a young reporter, George Willard. Tom Willard and his sickly wife Elizabeth run a shabby hotel. Tom is a person of regrets, trying to live through his son George, who has become a small-town reporter. Elizabeth's serious health problems seem to affect nobody but herself and the family doctor.

Many of the people are unhappy and they all present their sensitive stories of their imagination. Individually they cluster around George to report their own histories, at which time these sad tales are revealed. It is difficult to imagine so many tales in one little town. Although the people have simple dreams, none of them are fulfilled. The language is powerful and the book is worth reading.

5

Riders of the Purple Sage
Zane Grey (1872–1939)
New York: Harper Brothers, 1912

The pure goodness of Jane Withersteen and incarnate evil in the form of the elders of the Mormon Church are set in the richly hued country of sage and rock. Wealthy rancher Jane is condemned by her church for refusing marriage to Bishop Tull and for being good to the wrong people: Gentiles as well as Mormons. She is beset by the loss of her cattle (presumably by rustlers), her prized horses, and her Mormon riders and she must fire her household staff who is spying on her. Her main support is the mysterious gunman Lassiter who rides into town with his own agenda of hate toward Mormons. Jane's challenges: tame the black-clad gunfighter and keep her religious beliefs while maintaining her independence.

A secondary tale concerns Venters, one of Jane's supporters and ex-foremen, and a female masked rider with the rustlers. There's plenty of action with wild chases on horseback, gunshots in the night, stampeding cattle, and a pristine form of love. But the dominant theme is the majestic land with its harsh beauties in the mesa and canyon country (a land the Monkey Wrench Gang fights to take back from its human despoilers sixty years later). An obvious book for the movies, but so well written that one can see the scenery in the mind's eye. The first Western ever to hit the best-seller lists.

You Know Me Al
Ring Lardner (1885–1933)
New York: Scribners, 1916

Sent up to the major leagues, Jack Keefe remains a "busher" and naive rube in the big city. In a series of (sometimes insulting) letters to his friend Al back home, he tells of his pitching prowess, his female conquests and marriage, his unreasonable expenses (he never tips and doesn't admit how cheap he is)—all with his somewhat illiterate spelling based on sound. He has a pitching talent, knows that no one can "learn" him anything, knows he is never wrong and the fault always belongs to another, and is rather stupid but funny (funny in the way another character describes him—Jack provides a laugh when he doesn't even know he's being funny).

Lardner, noted as a Chicago sportswriter who also wrote short stories, made American prose talk. He wrote in ordinary speech, having an amazing ear for the spoken word. At the time of *Al's* publication, using colloquial language was quite a surprise to the reading populace. Thousands responded with joy to Lardner's early baseball stories that became this book because they heard their own voices coming from the printed page. Every line Lardner wrote was American English as befitted the character speaking, e.g., crude, egoistic baseball pitcher Jack writing to Al. His technique was emulated (not always with as much success) by novelists who followed. His novel has humor, irony, and a dab of acerbity.

The Magnificent Ambersons
Booth Tarkington (1869–1946)
New York: Doubleday, 1918

One of the most famous American writers of his time, Tarkington was successful and twice awarded the Pulitzer but is relatively unknown today. He writes of a midwestern nineteenth century, serene pastoral town that changes into a dirty, industrial city of the twentieth century—all in the name of progress, beginning with the advent of the automobile. The third-generation Amberson, George Amberson Minafer (an insufferable bastard when not being a consummate ass), must somehow be forced to adapt to the adjustments in his town and in his family's reputation and fortune.

Although somewhat stilted in language, but with sardonic wit and George's rather implausible reasons for destroying the woman he loves most (his mother), the book is worth reading for its turn of the century setting and the development of the characters. You care what happens to them with the decay of the once grand and peaceful town. A contrived, somewhat happy ending!

The 1920s
The Roaring Twenties

The Nineteenth Amendment gives women the right to vote.

Flagpole sitting, goldfish swallowing, the Charleston, jazz, and speak-easies mark the era.

KDKA begins the first regular radio broadcasts.

The weekly newsmagazine *Time* begins.

John Scopes is tried in the Scopes Monkey Trial for teaching evolution.

In the Harlem Renaissance, African-American writers, artists, and musicians flourish.

Bootlegger and gangster Al Capone rules Chicago.

Charles Lindbergh completes the first solo transatlantic flight.

The Book-of-the-Month club begins.

The first major motion picture with sound, *The Jazz Singer,* opens, and the first cartoon with sound features Mickey Mouse.

Black Tuesday, the stock market crash, heralds the Great Depression of the 1930s.

The first disposable tissue is developed under the trade name Kleenex; the Band-Aid is developed.

Early Autumn: A Story of a Lady
Louis Bromfield (1896–1956)
New York: Grosset & Dunlap, 1926

The Pentlands are a family who have been the backbone of a community, a family in which the men married wives for thrift and house-wifely virtues rather than for beauty, a family solid and respectable and full of honor. It is a tribe magnificent in its virtue and its strength, even at times in its intolerance and hypocrisy.

The strongest of the family, although related only by marriage, is Olivia, confidant of her father-in-law John; trapped in a loveless marriage to a pedantic bore, Anson; occasionally recognized by the insane appellation "her"; protective of her sickly young son Jack and coming-of-age daughter Sybil; and tolerant of the busybody Aunt Cassie. Enter distant relation Sabrine after a twenty-year absence—a schemer and hater who wishes only harm to the Pentlands. Next is the arrival of Michael O'Hara who, without education, money, or influence, has climbed from his humble beginnings to become "one of the great men of New England, a country which had once been the tight little paradise of people like the Pentlands." The elements for crisis and disaster mixed with the revelation of scandal from the past are in place. A beautifully written, well-plotted story with memorable characters, and a Pulitzer Prize winner worth reading and enjoying.

Death Comes for the Archbishop
Willa Cather (1873–1947)
New York: Knopf, 1927

A beautiful story, beautifully told! Father Latour (based on the real-life Archbishop Lamy) becomes the first Bishop of New Mexico with his fellow French seminarian, Father Vaillant (based on Bishop Machebeuf) as his cleric. Latour graced the beginning of an era and a vast new diocese with a fine personality. Vaillant rode the circuit as a much-loved missionary to various Indian tribes, Mexicans now Americans by conquest, and in his last assignment to the goldfields of Colorado. Cather draws a sympathetic portrait of the Mexicans of all castes, the Navajo and Pueblo Indians, and even the former Spanish priests who attempt to thwart the new bishop assigned by Rome. She graphically portrays the hardships as the priests travel great distances on the backs of mules to bring the word of God to the isolated believers.

But the main character is the unbelievable natural world of New Mexico and Arizona; the descriptions of the magnificent landscapes, the vagaries of weather, and ever the sky, a landscape that the Archbishop cannot leave to retire to his native France. To anyone who knows the desert it is gloriously described; to the unknowing a new world is truly revealed. A book for all ages celebrating the joy of life and still selling more than twenty thousand copies a year!

An American Tragedy

Theodore Dreiser (1871–1945)
New York: Boni and Liverwright, 1925

A work of fiction based on an actual New York murder case, this book tells the story of Clyde Griffiths, son of Kansas City street evangelists. This type of missionary upbringing is difficult for any child, especially when father Asa believes that God will provide. And as Clyde and his siblings are well aware, God seems to provide only poverty. Asa is more inclined to save the world than his own family.

As soon as he is old enough, Clyde begins working as a bellhop in a prominent hotel. For the first time in his life, he is a normal teenager with friends, some money in his pocket, and a chance for romance. This all changes when he and his friends have an accident in a car, taken without permission, and a young girl is killed. He flees to St. Louis for a time and then Clyde goes to work for a wealthy uncle in a New York factory. He is uncomplaining but lonely and eventually is promoted to foreman. Clyde is admonished that he is not to socialize with the factory workers, but in his forlornness, he is attracted to Roberta Alden, a young girl who works in the factory, and soon they begin a relationship. But he soon falls in love with Sondra Finchley, a wealthy socialite who seems to represent all that he wishes for in a wife. When Roberta announces that she is pregnant, she demands that Clyde take care of her.

Clyde plans to murder her and takes her to a lake resort where he intends to fake a boating accident. When they are on the lake, Clyde lacks the courage to complete the plan. The boat is overturned by accident and Clyde swims away, leaving Roberta to drown. Through extensive detective work he is finally apprehended. Clyde is arrested and, after a lengthy trial, condemned to death. This story has twice been made into a movie.

So Big
Edna Ferber (1887–1968)
New York: Doubleday, 1924

Sometimes you get what you want. "So Big" Dirk De Jong, with his mother's support, rises from his near-poverty background at High Prairie, Illinois, to wealth and society. Selina began as a naive, ill-trained teacher in her teens, and marries farmer Pervus De Jong, who dies a few years later, leaving her with one child and almost worthless farmland. Selina must do a man's work to eke a living from the farm and give her son the opportunities she wants for him.

Although trained as an architect, Dirk switches to a more lucrative position in banking. His mother Selina works an unforgiving farm and is almost broken by hard labor, but prevails. Selina, in one of her infrequent rebukes of her beloved son bemoans, "You don't get the full flavor of life," as she has in her adopted Dutch farm community.

Edna Ferber is expressing the belief that the good honest man works the soil, while prospering in an urban setting (here Chicago) corrupts the soul. This is a tale that is now almost a cliché having been told repeatedly although often not as well by later authors.

The Great Gatsby
F. Scott Fitzgerald (1896–1940)
New York: Scribners, 1925

To read Fitzgerald is to revel in the English language. His descriptions are vivid and sparse, using precise, evocative words to provide his setting and his plot. Gatsby the mysterious, the enigma, in love with the vacuous Daisy, characterizes the very rich of the 1920s. Fitzgerald shows the emptiness of the lives of shallow individuals who cannot even respond to the needless deaths of people they touch.

Fitzgerald became the voice of the Jazz Age with its flappers, bootleggers, lawnparties, and "crack-ups"—he helped invent it and told us when the doomed party was over. A difficult choice over *Tender Is the Night*; *Gatsby* has been called "short and perfect." In the 1990s some three hundred thousand copies were sold annually, and many consider *Gatsby* the finest American novel of the century.

Smoky, the Cowhorse
Will James (1892–1942)
New York: Scribners, 1926

A well-told animal story will always attract readers. Smoky, a mouse-colored pony, is destined for adventure from birth on the open range until he returns to the only master he ever acknowledged, Clint of the old Rocking R. On the range Smoky receives his early education before he meets the cowboy Clint, who tags him, makes him his own, and helps establish his reputation as one of the greatest cow ponies known. The life of the Far West—the open ranges, the ranch, the rodeo, and the desert—is told largely through the eyes of the horse. One enjoys with the horse his wild life on the range, his terror and struggle against man, his growing love and ability for the work of a cow pony. His life is active and adventurous. When Smoky is later mistreated by the half-breed, he becomes embittered and infamous as a bucking bronco that won't be ridden by any man.

Smoky's career is told in an informal, consciously uncultured style, which has its charm. Will James knew and loved horses: "To me, the horse is man's greatest, most useful, faithful and powerful friend." The book, written in a time of popularity for western fiction, stands out as a biography of a real and appealing character who has a mind and a heart all his own.

Accompanying the text are excellent drawings by Will James that capture both the action of the story and the appeal of Smoky. Usually considered a young adult book, it can be a pleasant evening's reading for any adult.

Babbitt
Sinclair Lewis (1885–1951)
New York: Harcourt Brace, 1922

Lewis's main character has entered the English language. According to Webster's *Third New International Dictionary of the English Language* (1967): "Babbitt: a person (as a business or professional man), who conforms unthinkingly and complacently to prevailing middle-class standards of respectability, who makes a cult of material success, and who is contemptuous of or incapable of appreciating artistic or intellectual values."

Babbitt is the conniving, successful real estate man from Zenith—a booster, in later terms "a good ole boy," an ugly figure, a social climber, a total conformist who uses all the current slang and catchwords. He can receive his self-esteem and his power in the community only from others; thus he is loyal to whoever serves his need at the moment. He is an opportunist in both business and domestic affairs. Although outwardly the bluff, hearty booster, inwardly he recognizes his emptiness of soul and at times has a vague feeling of dissatisfaction with this travesty of living. He even confesses to his son Ted at the book's end: "I've never done a single thing I've wanted to in my whole life! I don't know I've accomplished anything except just get along."

This is a sordid picture of the worst in American ways, thought, and speech at that moment in history, with its vulgarity and noise, its aimless rush, its motor and movie madness, and its spiritual emptiness. It is a satire of the American businessman that has its moments of ludicrous comedy. A book that is and will continue to be read, analyzed, and critiqued but a book that can just be read and appreciated.

Archy and Mehitabel
Don Marquis (1878–1937)
Garden City: Doubleday, 1927

It is humorous verse and not strictly a novel, but as Mehitabel would say "wothchell wothchell." It's fiction, cleverly written, and a delight to read. *The Lives and Times of Archy and Mehitabel*, the omnibus edition (1940) is composed of three books: *Archy and Mehitabel, Life of Mehitabel,* and *Archy Does his Part*, published respectively in 1927, 1933, and 1935. Although written by Archy for Don Marquis's *Sun Dial* columns in the first third of the century, there is a timeless quality that has the same appeal today as when they were written.

Mehitabel is morally careless, the alley cat who, by her own statement, is always the lady but whose actions disprove her words in the eyes of Archy, the cockroach, a reincarnated verse–libre poet. The presentation of all lowercase without punctuation, because Archy must hurt himself at the keys and cannot use the shift key on the typewriter, adds to the fun, along with the special illustrations by George Herriman, most noted for his cartoons of Krazy Kat.

Archy writes disparagingly about Mehitabel, who was once Cleopatra, but is too often distracted by the most disreputable tomcats and whose motto is "toujours gai" and "there's a dance or two in the old dame still" as she lives out her ninth life. He philosophizes about human attitudes toward the ugly as opposed to the beautiful in the insect and rodent world. He interviews the mummy of an Egyptian pharaoh, visits the tomb of Napoleon, discusses compassionate marriage, and modern statesmanship, and progressively becomes more pessimistic about civilization in general and the United States in particular. Read in segments over time, Marquis's book reveals much about his and our times with a special quixotic humorous twist.

The Sound and the Fury
William Faulkner (1897–1962)
New York: Random House, 1929

How can you select just one Faulkner book, and how can you write just a few words when so many millions have already been written? If you like his stream-of-consciousness, convoluted style challenging innovations of unexplained time shifts, and intimate depictions of strong characters set in the South, almost any selection of his major works will do, as the prizes awarded to his writings testify. Chronology is deliberately flaunted; the mind is the determinant about what is happening. Faulkner can be difficult to read until you go with the rhythm without carefully analyzing what is happening at the moment. It will all become clear and it is worth the effort. There is a plot of sorts but characterization and the words—how they are formed, how one follows the other, how they sound, how they flow together—are most important. Faulkner is concerned with time and memory and he has a tragic story to tell.

Sound and Fury, Faulkner's own favorite, is told through the eyes of the man-child Benjy and his two brothers—the highly intelligent, sensitive Quentin and the evil Jason—and the black cook Dilsey. Each section has its own style to fit the narrator, from Benjy's simple impressions and images to Quentin's obsessions and Jason's single-minded viciousness. Only Dilsey has a straightforward narrative, which brings order out of the disorder of the Compsons. Through the participants and onlookers you see the Compson family decline with black humor.

The Treasure of the Sierra Madre
B. Traven (1890–1969)
New York: Knopf, 1927

A great adventure story with the age-old theme of gold and greed. Good and evil are rewarded or punished as appropriate. The superb, oft times brutal descriptions place the reader clearly in the Mexican country-side. Much of the story is told by its participants, but the dialogue is often stilted and not befitting the rough characters. Occasional diatribes against the evil side of the Catholic Church and the big, outside companies also mar the story line. Even with these faults the reader continues for the well-written, "what happens next" adventure, fascinated with the events of the gold seekers as they labor for treasure and morally disintegrate before the reader's eyes.

Like other twentieth-century novels relating a good story, it becomes almost impossible to separate book from movie or book character from movie actor. The 1948 John Ford production with Humphrey Bogart as the old man Howard dominates the reader's senses.

The Age of Innocence
Edith Wharton (1862–1937)
New York: Appleton, 1920

The game of life is played by the traditional and arbitrary rules set by 1880s–1890s New York society. Newland Archer moves comfortably through his prescribed roles as he woos and plans to wed acceptable May Weiland. He is seriously distracted and his world is forever altered by the return to New York of the Countess Ellen Olenska, somewhat mysterious and a non-conformist. For Newland to defy the social order that counted most the values of loyalty, decency, honesty, fidelity, and adherence to moral com-mitment was to disturb the foundations of this society. But the enormous temptation by Ellen is there and he realizes that what has filled his days is like a parody of life.

This is a classic story of thwarted love set against gas-lit streets with formal dances in the ballrooms of stately brownstones, gentlemen's clubs, and society people who abhor scandal in any form. There is Cen-tral Park, the new Metropolitan Museum, and there is Newport, the summer extension of New York with its archery contests and horse shows—the watering-place banalities all remembered by the author rather affectionately.

The characters are real—you know their thoughts and yearnings and the price they are paying for these yearnings. The sensitive and expert dramatization of place heightens the conflict between the social and the personal and the moral issues involved. It is a compelling account of the age of innocence and is worthy of a few quiet tears shed by the reader at the ending. A Pulitzer Prize winner.

The Bridge of San Luis Rey
Thornton Wilder (1897–1975)
New York: Boni, 1927

Capricious fate? Or Divine Intervention takes five disparate people to their deaths on a tiny footbridge in Peru? Either we live by accident and die by accident, or we live by plan and die by plan. A tightly woven story with an intricate weaving of plot and characters answers the question for Brother Juniper who witnessed the tragedy. The impact of the tragedy deeply impressed the Peruvians but only the good monk sets out to discover the truth. The description of the disintegration of the bridge should also impress the reader and make one pause before crossing any such structure in the future.

A finely crafted book that reveals the secrets of half a dozen men, women, and children and leads them to their fate. Wilder's novel won him the Pulitzer Prize.

Look Homeward, Angel
Thomas Wolfe (1900–1938)
New York: Scribners, 1929

Born in 1900, the youngest of nine children, six of whom survive infancy. So begins the story of Eugene Gant, an autobiographical novel of Thomas Wolfe set in Altamont, North Carolina. Father Oliver is a strange character, a heavy drinker who can become violent when he's into the bottle. Eugene is fascinated by his father, his anger, his love of craftsmanship, and his rhetoric. A stonecutter by trade, Oliver settles in Altamont as he is roaming the country. He meets Eliza, they marry, and the children arrive in rapid succession. The family dynamics are extreme, with stresses and competition between the father and the mother and among the six siblings. After Eugene wins an essay contest, several of the teachers invite him to attend a new private school. He shows great academic promise, which again sets him apart from the rest of the children. However, everything must be weighed and measured where finances are concerned.

This is the coming-of-age story of Eugene, whose desire to experience life to the fullest takes him from his rural home. Eventually, Eugene goes away to college and Eliza and Oliver attend his graduation. He returns to Altamont with great dread and the family is inevitably feuding. Then, as Mr. Gant becomes frail and Eliza ignores his needs, the family is again divided. Determined to attend Harvard and finally end his ties with his family, Eugene goes off alone after his mother promises to pay for one year there. This book reflects author Thomas Wolfe's own childhood. He died when he was only thirty eight, but it is safe to state he saw more than a lifetime of family discord.

The 1930s
The Great Depression

The Dust Bowl ravages the Midwest.

The Social Security Act is Passed.

Jesse Owens wins four gold medals at the Berlin Olympics.

The yo-yo becomes a popular toy.

Sinclair Lewis is the first American to win the Nobel Prize for Literature.

Parker Brothers releases the game Monopoly.

Frances Perkins is the first woman to hold a cabinet post.

Three-year-old Shirley Temple makes her motion picture debut.

The man-made wonders Boulder Dam and the Golden Gate Bridge open.

Disney's *Snow White and the Seven Dwarfs* is the first full-length animated movie.

Germany invades Poland, launching World War II.

New patents are issued for a parking meter, nylon, Revlon nail enamel, the ballpoint pen, and Scotch tape.

Anthony Adverse
Hervey Allen (1889–1949)
New York: Farrar, 1933

Anthony comes into the world as a result of his mother, Maria's, liaison with another man. After Maria dies in childbirth, her husband, Don Luis, abandons the baby at a convent, where the nuns raise him. Bestowed the name of Anthony by the nuns because he has arrived on that saint's feast day, and is nurtured by the religious women and parish priest, Anthony is banished from the convent after he unintentionally views one of the nuns without her headband.

The book tracks Anthony through Spain, Cuba, New Orleans, and other places. His adventures are frequent, his romantic interludes even

18

more frequent. While in the American wilderness, he is captured first by Indians, then escapes, and is eventually recaptured by Mexican soldiers (in what is now Texas) and imprisoned. But there is a happy ending when a benevolent woman visits the prison as an act of mercy, meets Anthony, and they eventually marry. The book would have made a good TV miniseries.

The Good Earth
Pearl S. Buck (1892–1973)
New York: Day, 1931

Land is the key to prosperity for Wang Lung, a poor, honest, hardworking peasant in turn-of-the-century rural China. He and his selfless wife, O-lan, fight poverty and the perils of floods, famine, and tragedy with backbreaking labor to feed their fast-growing extended family while trying to set aside a "bit of silver" to acquire land for planting. Against all odds they succeed, with most of the benefits going to the next generation. Even the ancient Wang Lung rarely has peace within his own highly respected, wealthy family.

Against a background of sweeping revolutionary change in early twentieth-century China, Buck has woven a moving epic and provided insights into the ways and customs of a peasant class of Asiatic people rarely understood by Americans. Her characters are real people struggling against almost insurmountable odds, while the political and social upheavals and distant rumblings have little effect on ordinary people in the countryside.

Although sometimes criticized as an American attempting to write about the Chinese, Buck wrote from her own familiarity and with admiration for these people. She tells a universal story of human struggle, but *The Good Earth* is unique to its setting with real, not artificial, characters. That which differs in the Oriental outlook on life is not explained but is simply accepted as part of this well-told story. A Pulitzer Prize winner.

The Postman
Always Rings Twice
James M. Cain (1892–1977)
New York: Grosset & Dunlap, 1934

All the unexpected twists and turns are here, making the story suspenseful. Unfortunately, the "unexpected" are now clichés, but reading an expert's handling of this sparse—not a word-wasted—plot is still enjoyable. It does not detract from the story of two rather unsavory characters (and the author makes no attempt to elicit sympathy for them) that you can predict what is going to happen to them. Justice and goodwill triumph over crime and evil.

Another book that is difficult to separate from the well-made movie starring John Garfield and sex goddess Lana Turner reflects the author's years as a Hollywood scriptwriter. Related by amoral, hard-boiled, tough guy Frank Chambers, the story is told through conversation reflecting the violence and eroticism, which got the book banned in Boston. Tame by today's standards, the story still sizzles and horrifies as the characters, because of a misbegotten sense of romantic love, plot the murders that will guarantee their future together.

Tobacco Road
Erskine Caldwell (1903–1987)
New York: Grosset, 1932

What totally disgusting, pitiful, naive characters, who, were they not so tragic, would be completely laughable. Jeeter Lester, his wife Ada, daughter Ellie May, son Dude, and the old grandmother comprise a family of sorts who is living in poverty on Tobacco Road in Georgia, a little less than human and a little better than animals. Their lives are consumed by what could be, if God wished, and in the meantime they starve, fight, and copulate.

The older children have run away to work in the mills, but Jeeter must stay to plant the cotton fields if only he can get seed cotton and guano. Enter Sister Bessie Rice (pushing forty) who wishes to marry sixteen year old Dude and presumably make him a preacher man, but in reality she seeks "sex." Dude concedes when Bessie spends $800 for a new car to be driven by Dude. The scenes with the car, which is quickly destroyed within a week, are humorous but the succeeding tragedies cause little emotional reaction from the reader. These are the ribald adventures of a shiftless family with other earthly men and women along the road. Caldwell gives the impression of absolute reality in a powerful novel of people ignorant of the civilization that both encompasses and ignores them. Their sexual adventures are treated with irreverence bordering on the burlesque.

The Big Sleep
Raymond Chandler (1888–1959)
New York: World Publishing, 1939

Clean, sparse, visually descriptive writing—each character is clearly delineated. You can see a movie in the smells, the tastes, and the scenes of 1930s Los Angeles. Photography is redundant to Chandler's depictions. Phil Marlowe has become a stereotype for a detective—hard-drinking, sexy, street-wise, smoking a cigarette, shooting down the bad guys, but with a strong moral, ethical streak. The bad guys wear black hats and kill each other, the cops are shady, and the women are blond lovable bimbos. But the real star is Southern California with its truly recorded vernacular, its smog, and its tarnished beauty reflected in the various lights of day.

The story is a melodrama with an exaggeration of violence and fear, and Marlowe is a crusading knight fighting both individual and social evil. He expresses his contempt for corrupt city administrations; crooked police; smut bookshops; phony yogis; and various drifters, grafters, pimps, and peepers. The book is about a social morality unlike what Chandler himself called the "comic books" of Mickey Spillane. All the people are vividly alive—even minor characters like bartenders, elevator men, and parking lot attendants. His major characters are gloriously real and all can be encountered on the streets of L.A. today.

Although he did not invent the hard-boiled murder story (even Chandler credited Dashiell Hammett), he crafted it to the heights of creative literature. He gave it an exaggerated reality, excitement, and a good dose of humor. He was a master of one-liners, which elicit laughter although they now seem quaint.

U.S.A. Trilogy
John Dos Passos (1896–1970)
New York: Harcourt Brace, 1930-36

A sprawling trilogy (each part can be read alone) chronicling the first thirty years of America's twentieth century in a unique interweaving of individual episodic fictions, accounts of major cultural figures, newspaper and newsreel headlines, and lyrics of popular songs. It consists of *The 42nd Parallel* (1930), *1919* (1932) and *The Big Money* (1936).

The fictional narrative is segmented by documentary and biography doing short solo turns: Dos Passos's technique mimics jazz as themes and characters surface, take center stage, and disappear only to surface and intersect later. The dozen or so major characters featured are a deliberately chosen societal cross-section but their stories, though the largest part of this scrapbook, are often less interesting than the shorter, fact-grounded selections that separate their narratives. The rhythm of the work and lightest prose is rather in the biographies—told in essentially free verse—and in the snippets of songs and headlines that convey the magnitude of the economic and social changes between the start of the century and the end of the 1920s. *USA* is classified as fiction, but its heart and chief reading pleasure is eyewitness journalism—and ferreting out the form in what at initial reading appears a random, unorganized mass and mixture of prose.

Drums Along the Mohawk
Walter Dumaux Edmonds (1903–1998)
Boston: Little Brown, 1936

The Mohawk Valley pioneers of 1776 had few defenses against the British forces in Canada and their Indian allies. Fictional Gil Martin brings his young bride Lana to isolated land at Deerfield, and as they struggle to clear the land, the Senecas burn them out. As the British and Indians threaten, the poorly conditioned, poorly trained, but well-intentioned militia mobilizes to augment the few colonials in the small stockades. The militia and regulars are finally tested in the battle of Oriskany, which they eventually win but with great losses. Appeals for regular troops are routinely denied and the Mohawk Valley inhabitants realize their main defense will be themselves.

Historical sagas with real people combined with fictional characters were popular in the mid-twentieth century. Edmonds attempts to be as faithful to the scene and time and place "as study and affection could help me to be." He depicts life as it was and the minutiae of living, including the weather, in its broader historical context. Original letters and documents are quoted to explain the horrifying events. The settlers are repeatedly harassed with destroyed settlements, while both the capital at Albany and the Congress at Washington, not recognizing local problems, turn away pleas for help. The forces on both sides commit atrocities, but although the people of the valley lose two-thirds of their fighting strength, they take hold and prevail. Outnumbered by well-equipped, trained troops, the farmers and their families win the final battle of the long war. They lay the foundations of a great and strong community.

Studs Lonigan: A Trilogy
James T. Farrell (1904–1979)
New York: Random House, 1935

Hangin' out with the gang, ditchin' school, fighting, experimenting with sex, occasionally fulfilling good intentions, working part-time for extra cash, sleeping late, arguing with parents, playing pool (video games), Studs Lonigan is a modern teenage boy growing up in a low-income urban environment. He knows he should be achieving some goal in life and he has impossible dreams of what he could be if only ... but he never quite gets started on his ambitions. The trilogy of *Young Lonigan* (1932), the *Young Manhood of Studs Lonigan* (1934) and *Judgment Day* (1935) is a sociological study of South Side Chicago in the 1920s and 1930s.

Vein of Iron
Ellen Glasgow (1874–1945)
New York: Harcourt Brace, 1935

A rather bland book for contemporary times. Ralph and Ada, childhood sweethearts at the beginning of the century, are thwarted from marriage, have a quick affair in which she becomes pregnant, and then are separated by World War I. Later they marry, have their usual family tragedies, suffer economic deprivation in the city in the 1930s, and finally return to Ironside in the Appalachians and the central characters of the book: the land and the stone house—the Manse. But it's worth reading for its descriptions of the Virginia high country and the strong delineation of most characters.

Running through six generations, the vein of iron derives from their belief in God and the austere Scotch-Presbyterian faith, and reflects the strength of the people from the first pioneer, John Mincastle, who wrested the land from the Indians to Ada, the strong heroine unbowing to adversity. Ada's extended family consists of her philosopher father, her grandmother still reflecting her pioneer inheritance, the crushed-by-circumstances southern belle mother, Mary Evelyn, from Tidewater Virginia, the family spinster, Aunt Meggie, and the colored folks like Aunt Abigail. All rise above the usual fictional stereotypes. The unemotional Ralph, the optimist turned cynic, is not as attractive to the reader as to Ada, who would love no other, and is simply too good for him.

Written during the height of her career, Glasgow was popular and widely read, with her everyday characters leading lives like her readers, and her strong women who overcome whatever fate befalls them.

The Maltese Falcon
Dashiell Hammett (1894–1961)
New York: Knopf, 1930

Sam Spade, on radio and television, became synonymous with the grubby private investigator, the hard-boiled detective. If you have doubts, in the first few pages he called his girl "Sweetheart" and "Angel," drank Bacardi straight, rolled his own cigarettes, and played hardball with the cops in a murder investigation. What are also now clichés are presented here in the physical, stereotypical descriptions of the cops, the bad guys and the good-looking (read sexy) female client who keeps lying. In spite of familiarity with this genre, the story is still fresh and suspenseful, truly a compliment to an author who has had so many imitators. He gave the American mystery story a distinct dialogue with a smart-mouthed, deadpan character with a slightly florid vocabulary, which in time would become a part of American fiction. As Raymond Chander wrote of him in

1944, "He was spare, frugal, hard-boiled, but he did over and over again what only the best writers can ever do at all. He wrote scenes that never seemed to have been written before." Problems are solved by violence or threats of violence—it's a macho, male chauvinist world with no doubt about evil and some ambiguity about good. Words are as effective a weapon as fists or guns.

As with other books successfully filmed, the *Maltese* characters will forever be Humphrey Bogart as a somewhat sanitized Sam Spade, Sydney Greenstreet in his first film appearance, and Peter Lorre as the faces of evil.

Lost Horizon
James Hilton (1900–1954)
New York: Morrow, 1933

A very British story set in the outposts of the great Empire in the 1930s, *Lost Horizon* was popular both as a novel and as a movie. (Hilton later took out naturalization papers in the U.S.). Its setting has entered the English language. "Shangri-La: imaginary mountain land depicted as a utopia ... a remote beautiful imaginary place where life approaches perfection (*Webster's Third Unabridged Dictionary*).

Four diverse people, three men and a woman missionary, are kidnapped in India and flown to Shangri-La to bolster the pool of people at the monastery located in a spectacular high-mountain, lush valley setting. All people live in perfect harmony. In time, two will accept their new life; one man will rebel; and one, the brilliant Conway who in the past has never quite lived up to others' expectations, will totally embrace the ways of the people of the hidden valley. But before he can accept his designated role, he must help the rebel escape, to the detriment of his own health; while he recovers from his physical and mental (primarily amnesiac) illness he will reveal his experiences to a disbelieving outside world that thinks him mad. An interesting tale of one man's vision of paradise.

The Late George Apley
John P. Marquand (1893–1960)
Boston: Little Brown, 1937

A remarkable story about a rather remarkable man trying to live by the guidelines set by his forebears in a changing world that no longer follows all the traditional rules. Quoting from letters, diaries, papers, and memos, a close friend at the request of Apley's son John writes a memoir to be privately printed for the extended family. Nothing is to be omitted, including a purported scandal that shadowed George's later years. The time period is 1866 to 1933; the place is Boston. The first Apley settled in Massachusetts in 1636 and the family prospered. George Apley is a man of privilege and wealth and has said of himself, "I am the sort of man I am, because environment prevented my being anything else." For the most part Apley behaves as a Brahmin in the city of Boston with its culture, class distinctions, virtues, and failings. George joins the correct clubs, serves on all the right boards, discreetly handles the family skeletons, but is threatened by the brash, takeover Irish politicos who become first his enemies and then his sympathizers. Through it all he is a decent, generous man.

Marquand's subtle ironic satire describes and presents without comment. His work has a lasting attraction, as the reader must draw his or her own conclusions. A Pulitzer Prize winner.

Gone with the Wind
Margaret Mitchell (1900–1949)
New York: Macmillan, 1936

Reading GWTW (as it is known) is like viewing a movie in your mind. The two media are inseparable—national mythology with some of the dialogue entering the vernacular. Vivian Leigh will forever be the saucy, indomitable, beautiful Scarlet O'Hara; Clark Gable the handsome "cad" Rhett Butler; Leslie Howard the shy Ashley Wilkes; Olivia de Haviland the optimistic, ever-forgiving Melanie; Hattie McDaniel the stalwart Mammy. The scenes of the Twelve Oaks ball with the brave Confederate dandies, the casualties, and the burning of Atlanta will always owe much to the Hollywood portrayal. But the book has much more to offer: expanded characterization, which gives depth to the plot;

fuller explanations of the whys of various actions; the overlying tragedy of the southern loss and reconstruction. There is not a sympathetic Yankee in the lot. The hardships and the will to survive against all odds and by any means are poignantly written.

Margaret Mitchell became with her one book a great popular novelist, widely read in 1936, a Pulitzer Prize winner, and today a best-selling American novel. The book is a sweeping narrative of a lost world with bigger-than-life characters—a great story to be read and enjoyed. But don't bother with the sequel written some fifty years later.

Kitty Foyle
Christopher Morley (1890–1957)
Philadelphia: Lippincott, 1939

About the highest accolade Philadelphia ever received was the supposed epitaph of W. C. Fields: "All things considered I'd rather be in Philadelphia." Kitty Foyle grew up in this city in the 1910s and 1920s as well as with her aunt and uncle in Manitou, Illinois, and a proper Irish middle growing-up it was. Forced to drop out of college to nurse her widowed father, she meets and is courted by Wynnewood Strafford VI (Wyn) from the Main Line (Wealthyard), with a lineage going back seven generations in Pennsylvania. She finds employment in the depression years of the 1930s, and she and her friend Molly from Chicago are characterized as not the women of the covered wagon, but the women of the covered typewriter, the White-Collar Girl, the business sharecropper.

Can Kitty Foyle find happiness in the big city of New York and in her job in the cosmetics industry when Wyn marries Main Line? Will she ever find love? A true soap opera told by Kitty, tinged with post World War I nostalgia and the beginnings of the independent working girl who can be secure in herself, without a man. A hit movie starring Dennis Morgan and Ginger Rogers and a somewhat dated book that can still be enjoyed as a look at the 1920s and early 1930s from a working woman's viewpoint.

The Yearling
Marjorie Kinnan Rawlings (1896–1953)
New York: Scribners, 1938

Variously listed as an adult, juvenile, or young adult book, *The Yearling* is a novel for all ages and winner of the Pulitzer Prize for adult fiction in 1939. Struggling to earn a hard (but satisfying) living from the Florida Everglades (post Civil War) where man, like the animal, kills to eat, the Baxters are a self-sufficient family. Hunting and farming are their livelihood. Jody, the son, is the focus: learning to live and hunt in the beautifully described backwoods country, learning his world and its human and animal inhabitants. The Forrester's rip-roaring, hard-drinking nearest neighbors must unite with the Baxters for survival against nature's travails—unusual storms and wild beasts. And through all the hardships, Jody has Flag, the fawn, to love and tend. This picture of life so removed from modern patterns of living becomes universal in its revelations of simple, courageous people and their abiding beliefs. The dialect and the surroundings are exquisitely drawn for the reader, who becomes physically and emotionally there as both the deer and Jody mature. Other characters are memorable if not lovable: Penny, the father Buck one of the better Forresters, Fodder-wing, and Old Slewfoot.

For additional pleasure select the edition illustrated by N. C. Wyeth, who captures the feel and beauty of the Everglades. *The Yearling* was predicted to become a classic. If that means well read and well loved by many, it has achieved that status.

Northwest Passage
Kenneth Roberts (1885–1957)
New York: Doubleday, 1937

Some of the greatest heroes of America's frontier, Rogers' Rangers, fighting as American provincials in the British Army, could do what the regular troops could not: conquer the French and Indian enemy. As a result of successes, Rogers receives no backing from his British superiors in his search for a route across the northern land to connect the Atlantic and Pacific—the Northwest Passage.

Robert Rogers led the expedition against the Indian town of St. Francis in 1759. The story is told by Langdon Towne who joins the expedition to paint Indians realistically. Towne becomes like all other followers, a dedicated worshipper of Rogers when he leads the Rangers through hell and back again. The book has four distinct parts: the 1759 expedition, the interval in London where Rogers tries to get backing to seek the Northwest Passage and Towne studies painting, Rogers' career as governor of Michillimackinac, Roger's court martial and Towne's success as a painter. Rogers is larger than life and accomplishes the unbelievable, but with an ego that will not recognize its limitations and will destroy him. Here is a thrilling adventure and an account of the disintegration of character. This is vivid living history accurately portraying the hunger and desire of a nation about to break westward into new land in pre-revolutionary America.

The Grapes of Wrath
John Steinbeck (1902–1968)
New York: Viking, 1939

Considered a classic of American literature and justly so, assigned in college classes, and on all the must-read lists if you are "educated." But don't be put off by its promotion. It's a good book, an important book, with a tragic story that relates the times of the Dust Bowl and the continuing Depression of the 1930s. The Joad family represents all the "Okies" in battered jalopies, carrying their meager earthly goods and headed for the promised-land of California and work. A heartbreaker of a story—you so want something to go right but life is not like that in those terrifying years. While the Joads' sad misadventures exemplify the traveling "homeless," Steinbeck interjects other tales and the national background in succeeding chapters amongst the Joad family narrative. He depicts a period that was possibly the most terrifying in our nation's history since the Civil War. The misery of the Joads includes the death of family members, the desertion of a son, a stillborn baby, persecution by townspeople and police and when work is available, exploitation by California farmers.

Steinbeck writes with anger and indignation at the social cruelty of the period but the book has touches of humor as well as bitterness. The characters are coarse and rough with a bittersweet tenderness as they learn to survive. There is a felt emotional quality. Out of the travails of the Joads and their repeated dealings with the hard realities of an America clearly divided between the haves and have-nots, there is an intensely human drama—tragic but heartfelt in its insistence on human dignity. One of the great books of American fiction, a Pulitzer Prize winner, and a book that defines the Great Depression in words as the Farm Security Administration did in photographs.

The Day of the Locust
Nathaniel West (1903–1940)
New York: Random House, 1939

Only in Hollywood, where reality and facade are often indistinguishable! West depicts the oddities of the general population with such surreal characters as a cocky dwarf; a landlady whose hobby is funerals; a dying vaudeville comic; a voluptuous teenage extra; a repulsive child actor with his even more repulsive mother; and the obsessed, all-consuming fans. These are all seen through the presumably normal eyes and stable mind of a bookkeeper from Iowa hoping for a career as a set designer. This is a violent story, depicting a rage against life with bitter laughter, mad hallucinations, and savage surreal disillusionment and cynicism. Violence triumphs!

Written with derisive humor in a sparse style; the economy of language only heightens the horror. A true Hollywood gothic novel and forerunner of the later black humorists. Clifton Fadiman proclaimed it "an unpleasant, thoroughly original book."

The 1940s
World War II

Germany takes the offensive against France; emergency evacuation from Dunkirk.

M&M candies are developed for the U.S. Army, to "melt in your mouth, not in your hands."

The Japanese bomb Pearl Harbor and the United States declares war.

Nisei (Japanese–Americans) internment.

GI Bill of Rights passed.

Oklahoma! is new musical theater with lyrics incorporated into the plot.

Developed as the Manhattan Project in New Mexico, the atomic bomb is dropped on Hiroshima and Nagasaki, and the Japanese surrender.

Chuck Yeager becomes the first human to break the sound barrier.

Numerous innovations include the electric razor, first stereo system, Kodachrome film, garbage disposal, releasable ski bindings, fluorescent lighting, Teflon, jet engine, nylon, permanent-press fabrics, cake mixes, and Tupperware.

United Nations formed in San Francisco.

Jackie Robinson breaks baseball's color barrier.

The Marshall Plan is instituted.

The Man with the Golden Arm
Nelson Algren (1909–1981)
New York: Doubleday, 1949

Isn't it ironic that a man can return unscathed from a war yet get seriously wounded on the streets of Chicago? This book features a multitude of characters, but Frankie Machine is the main personality. His name is derived from his ability to deal cards at a record pace in a gaming hall. Not a bad man, but one inclined to constantly lose the battle with his addictions. He is surrounded by other characters, all of whom have outlandish nicknames, such as Sparrow, Molly-O, Blind Pig, Nifty Louie, and

Drunken John to name a few. And all have a love for the bottle and are distinct personalities in their own right.

Frankie lives with his wife Sophie. Early in their marriage, Frankie was driving drunk when he crashed into an obstruction and Sophie was seriously injured. After a few days she develops a paralysis and after that is never able to walk again. She spends her time in their small flat, rolling her wheelchair back and forth and continuously reminding her husband of what he has done to her. It is a heavy price for anyone to deal with, but to his credit, Frankie does provide her with the bare necessities.

When one of the bar's patrons is murdered, Frankie and his friend Sparrow become the prime suspects. At that point both men go into hiding and disappear from the neighborhood. Simultaneously Sophie is hospitalized with a severe mental disorders. The ending is unexpected and leaves the reader with the sense that some people can damage themselves more than the artillery from any foreign enemy. Frank Sinatra starred in the movie.

Kings Row
Henry Bellamann (1882–1945)
New York: Sun Dial Press, 1940

Things are not what they seem behind the facades of the pleasant town of Kings Row. The hidden secrets of some of the town's more prominent citizens will explode in horror and tragedy, and some will have terrible effects without the townspeople ever knowing the real cause.

Murder, suicide, incest, deliberate physical mutilation, and insanity will shatter the peaceful scene. All this is gradually revealed by the young boy Parris Mitchell, grown into manhood as a community outsider, with his idealism and integrity. In spite of his attempt to break all ties with his childhood, he will return to his roots in Kings Row as a doctor and psychiatrist. In addition to the inner turmoil, the town itself will change in response to the turn of the century from a sedate village to a small industrial town with suburbs.

The total effect of the book is the piling on of the ever-increasing, revealed horrors; the novel is read for its excitement and melodrama rather than for its underlying philosophy and indictment of small-town vulgarity, meanness, and criminality. A forerunner of Grace Metalious's *Peyton Place* (1956), *Kings Row* was the popular "potboiler" of the 1940s, written with more discreet descriptions and implied moral lessons required in novels of its time.

This Side of Innocence
Taylor Caldwell (1900–1985)
New York: Scribners, 1946

Another "potboiler" of the 1940s, well written with clearly delineated characters. New York playboy Jerome Lindsey returns to post-Civil War Hilltop in Riversend to protect his and his sister's future inheritance from his father's adopted son, Alfred. Although chafing from the boredom of a small town, Jerome amuses himself by falling in love with Amalie, Alfred's future bride and a woman with a past. This is a basis for disaster.

Jerome and Alfred become deadly enemies. Alfred, though deeply in love, punishes his bride for her sins, and the aging father Mr. Lindsey and daughter Dorothea and Alfred's crippled son Philip are consumed by the feud. The family split spills over into the community as Alfred inherits the management of the family bank and clings to tradition. Jerome founds a new bank based on progressive business practices; economics couched in humanitarian terms and invests in the growing laboring class. Although essential to the climax of the story, the concepts behind the competing banks result in rather simplistic discussions concerning the future of an industrial America and the care of its workers versus the past serene, pastoral life of the elite and its downtrodden poor. Still a good book; the reader can scan the tedious pages.

The Ox-Bow Incident
Walter Van Tilburg Clark (1909–1971)
New York: Vintage, 1940

No good guys in white hats, no bad guys in black hats, just real human guys riding out to right a wrong. Will they be a legal posse or a lynch mob when they find three rustlers and murderers? These are men doing their duty as they see it and expressing their innermost thoughts as they ride. They have listened to some of the best arguments presented in "down-home" terms of the need for justice and law. The book and the film, starring Henry Fonda, are intense, even though you guess the outcome, hoping the three men (who aren't totally believable as innocents) accused of rustling and murder will be saved. So much for the rule of "Judge Lynch."

This is a tale of primitive revenge set in the little cattle town of Bridger's Wells, Nevada in the 1880s. Tempers and emotions are high over rustlings and a perceived murder, culminating in the gang to round up the criminals. In a remote valley called the Ox Bow they come across three sleeping men. After a summary trial, they lynch them but discover afterwards that they are not the real culprits. The narrative is developed with remarkable tension but more important is the revealing of the motives and mental states of those involved. This has made the book a well-deserved American classic and, with the possible exception of *The Virginian,* the best-known novel of the American West.

The Keys of the Kingdom
A. J. Cronin (1896–1981)
Boston: Little Brown, 1942

A tragic youth turns Francis Chisholm toward the Catholic priesthood. Although a believer, he is an independent and liberal thinker, which often puts him in conflict with the members of the hierarchy and leaves him with the more undesirable assignments. In spite of adversity, he maintains a mission for thirty years in interior China where he must fight famine, flood, lack of supplies and support from the Mother Church, and guerrillas in the hills. He keeps his faith and slowly wins over the nuns working with him in spite of his unconventional ways. He becomes well loved by his community and teaches toleration as the highest virtue. His efforts offer an excellent lesson in faith, compassion, and trust in God, and portray a distinct contrast between the humble servant attempting to serve his people and their needs and their pompous bishop and abbess. At the end Francis Chisholm, a good man lame and weary but still indomitable, finally returns to spend his remaining years in his native Scotland.

Beautifully written in a dramatic style, Cronin's book is based on questions that deeply involve the faiths of many people; it evokes thought and possibly discussion even in our age. In one sense this is a book of propaganda on the futility of organized religion, which deals with eternal and redemptive values. Yet it should not be read as a moral treatise, but as an adventure story with exciting, melodramatic action.

The Robe
Lloyd C. Douglas (1877–1951)
Boston: Houghton Mifflin, 1942

Tribune Marcellius Lucan Gallio, son of the honored and honorable Senator Marcus Lucan Gallio, is sent on his first assignment by the vicious, petty and insane leadership of Rome. While stationed at the villainous port city of Minoa, Marcellius's company is ordered to escort to their crucifixion two thieves and an unusual Galilean who has been gathering crowds to hear him talk about a new religion. Marcellius through lots becomes the owner of the Galilean's robe and in a drunken orgy puts it on. He is struck by a mental affliction and bodily illness, and accompanied by his Greek slave, the well-educated Demetrius, he returns home. As he is recovering, both he and Demetrius are fated to learn of this crucified man and what he stood for. They travel to meet the followers of Jesus, and Demetrius becomes a convert.

Here is the story of Jesus told by a disbelieving but intelligent young Roman who risks his life to learn of this strange man's power and to find himself. It is a tale of adventure and a love story played out against the background of a corrupt Roman Empire led by insane emperors.

The wartime paper shortage in 1942, when the book was first published, meant that not enough copies could be printed to meet the popular demand. It was released five years later in an enhanced format with accompanying paintings. Seen as a book fitting the demands of its time with its parallelism of a world gone mad and its assurances that good will prevail, it is still a readable and engrossing story.

The Big Sky
A. B. Guthrie, Jr. (1901–1991)
New York: Sloane, 1947

Inspired by one of Charles M. Russell's tales, Guthrie portrays Boone Caudill, the mountain man, as a runaway teenager who strikes out for the West in the 1830s and stays even as the land is being settled and the animals are fast disappearing. He is hopeful that the good times of freedom, hunting, fighting for one's very existence, and adventure will return.

The mountain man appears to be a mythical character. He is a unique and short-lived figure who lives in unprecedented isolation. He has to possess courage, strength, endurance, wiliness, pride, resourcefulness, and closeness to nature to survive. *The Big Sky* is a full-length portrait that shows how he came to be, how he lived and what for, and how and why he passed. He develops his skills as he learns his country, carrying his maps in his head and silence as a necessity for survival. He is a sympathetic human character with habits appropriate to his life and roams an unspoiled world of incomparable beauty. The descriptions of the wilderness and the immense distances of the Rockies help give the book a lasting quality. The book captures the feeling of the Rockies and has justifiably been called "one of the most authentic novels of the West ever written" (Bernard DeVoto). Obviously, Hollywood could not pass it up. And Montana is universally known as "Big Sky Country"!

For Whom the Bell Tolls
Ernest Hemingway (1899–1961)
New York: Scribners, 1940

No one does war better than Hemingway, whether it's his *Farewell to Arms,* simplistically described as a story of the Italian defeat at Caporetto in World War I, or his later masterpiece *For Whom the Bell Tolls,* written with equal brevity and spoken of as a story about the Spanish Civil War. In both you have touching love stories, skillfully written with extraordinary fidelity in the dialogue. Both are the stories of a lost generation wracked by war and European demoralization, a brittle world subject to collapse, told with a deep vein of pathos under good-humored cynicism. These narratives are reactions of young men to danger and the conflict of ideas and passions. Although World War I may have produced no better work of fiction than *Farewell*, Hemingway's passionate feeling for the tragic faces of love and war, *For Whom the Bell Tolls* exceeds in its descriptions of the camaraderie of man and his capacity for brutality.

Robert Jordan, an American committed to the Republican cause, joins the guerrillas to blow up an essential bridge. He is theoretically a communist, the most effective force in loyalist Spain, but is actually a westerner believing in life, liberty, and the pursuit of happiness. He is typical of Hemingway heroism, true to the code of courage in performance and stoic in the face of pain and adversity. Quite accidentally, one of the most touching and perfect love stories occurs between Jordan and Maria, his "rabbit," which, in spite of its tragic ending, is uplifting. The personalities with whom Jordan comes in contact are a remarkable group of fully realized human beings. These peasants are Jordan's closest friends and most dangerous enemies. A dramatic tale of human nature set in the intensity of war.

A Bell for Adano
John Hersey (1914–1993)
New York: Knopf, 1944

In World War II the town of Adano is occupied by Allied forces. Italian-American Major Victor Joppolo is named senior civil affairs officer, and he wants to rebuild the town with his own good instincts and democratic background. He tries to understand the people—the fishermen, the children, the cartmen, and the officials—who want a new freedom but need to retain their own customs. The spirit of the town was reflected by its beloved ancient bell, which has been melted down by the fascists to make gun barrels. Major Joppolo sets out to reconstruct the bell for Adano, facing surprising opposition from his superiors and certain political segments of the town. The story unfolds with humor and pathos. Words written on paper as charters and agreements are only as effective as the men enjoined to implement them.

John Hersey, journalist and war correspondent, captures the beginnings of rebuilding conquered territories by reflecting on a small Italian town as a microcosm of all the difficulties to follow. The efforts of one good man are not quite enough. With hope and despair as the red tape escalates, the townspeople await their cherished bell. Not a war story but an excellent reflection of the impact of World War II. A Pulitzer Prize winner for fiction in 1945.

Gentleman's Agreement
Laura Z. Hobson (1900–1986)
New York: Simon & Schuster, 1947

This is a book that makes one think, with its not-so-subtle portrayal of anti-Semitism. After returning from World War II, Phil Green (byline Schulyer Green) receives his first major assignment for *Smith's Weekly Magazine*, a five-part series on anti-Semitism. As he settles into his New York apartment, he grapples with both the concept and how to make the subject interesting to readers. Because he is little known to his colleagues and is in a new environment, he subtly reveals that he is Jewish and plays the role, waiting to see what will happen. He is subjected to both overt and subtle discrimination. To his dismay his family—mother, married sister, and young son—are also affected, and the sharpness of the pain of anti-Semitism permeates his life and remains with him. The swift-moving events issue a powerful plea for toleration and moderation.

The book is not just a sermon; it is a good story. The necessary stereotypical characters are given life by the author: the desk clerk and owner denying reservations in a resort hotel; the fiancée who will learn to accept Phil and his campaign; the longtime best friend, Dave, also coping with the civilian world and its problems, which are magnified because he is Jewish. A thought-provoking book that, like the series Schulyer Green must have written, should attract readers with its story line.

Mr. Blandings
Builds His Dream House
Eric Hodgins (1899–1971)
New York: Simon & Schuster, 1946

A hilarious horror story in which city slicker meets rube and loses. Times have not changed. The vicissitudes of buying land and building a house met by Mr. Blandings in the late 1930s are still current today as the city person goes to the country seeking serenity, peace, and solitude—all worth the long commute to the city job. Bring the dollars up-to-date, and you have anyone who has tried to build his or her dream house with all its frustrations. The experience is universal regardless of geography. What can possibly go wrong will and does, and the costs just continue to escalate.

Well written, spontaneous humor, enjoyable to read with a serious foundation, the book has something important to say. Don't even take the first step of scanning the real estate ads without first meeting Mr. and Mrs. Blandings.

Raintree County
Ross Lockridge (1914–1948)
Boston: Houghton Mifflin, 1948

An unusual presentation of one day, July 4, 1892, with flashbacks in the life and often tragic loves of John Wickliff Shawnessy, the hero of *Raintree County*. The other leading character, who is intricately entwined with Shawnessy, is the county itself: its mysteries, its geography, its geological past, its history and prehistory, and its modern inhabitants within its man-made governmental structure. Over the years Shawnessy seeks the mythical raintree for the meaning of life. Although not in chronological order, the flashbacks gradually reveal the major incidents in Shawnessy's past over the middle and last half of the nineteenth century and provide suspense to the novel. Johnny reaches young manhood in the county and after suffering personal reverses and because of his own idealism, enlists in the Union Army and participates in Sherman's March to the Sea. He, at various times, seeks his fortune elsewhere, but unlike his close peers, he returns to his roots in Raintree County and from there can strongly believe in the future of the American Republic. His mentor and adult best friend, Professor Jerusalem Webster Stiles, provides the cynical devil's advocate and intellectual challenger to his somewhat unrealistic, optimistic beliefs.

The movie created from the events of the book rather than from its mystical and philosophical components, featured the rising young stars Montgomery Clift and Elizabeth Taylor. Although the movie was popular and well remembered, Hollywood could never do justice to this beautifully written, unusually constructed, interesting book.

The Heart Is a Lonely Hunter
Carson McCullers (1917–1967)
Boston: Houghton Mifflin, 1940

The mysterious man of mystical understanding, deaf-mute John Singer draws an unusual conglomerate of individuals reaching out to him from their islands of loneliness. The characters of small-town Georgia are sensitive, tomboyish Mick, seeking release through music; café owner and widower Biff; drifter, alcoholic carny worker Jake Blount, who sees himself as a reformer; and black Dr. Copeland, who can no longer passively accept the treatment of his race by the white community. Singer himself has his own hunt, for recognition by his beloved companion Antonopoulos, who has been institutionalized for mental illness. This is a quiet book of beauty, poetry, and power resulting in the inevitable heartbreak of people grimly working for their living without complaint but longing for more serenity, peace, and harmony. The only realization of their ideals the characters encounter is the stillness and serenity in the plain boardinghouse room of Singer, and even this is taken away from them.

Author McCullers shows remarkable perceptions (she was twenty-three when the book appeared) about the loneliness of the human heart and the societal indifference and hypocrisy that deepen it. Her work was praised by Richard Wright: that a white writer "for the first time in Southern fiction ... handle[s] Negro characters with as much ease and justice as those of her own race."

The Naked and the Dead
Norman Mailer (1923–)
New York: Rinehart, 1948

Here is the saga of a World War II U.S. Army reconnaissance platoon, somewhere on a Japanese-occupied island in the Pacific, presented in a tough, gritty, "mince no words" style. The language, considered offensive at the time of publication, fits the men using it and now seems mild. All the horrors of war are portrayed, as well as the boredom, the hard labor, the division and hatred between officers and GIs, the mud, the storms, the extremes of temperature, the jungle rot, and death. Each man, from the Tex-Mex scout to the general, is revealed through background pieces, his reactions to war as he faces his own mortality, and in some cases his hopes for the future. Over time the men's interior dramas emerge into the external conflict of the war.

In his first full-length work of fiction, Mailer captured the essence of the island invasion and the elaborate maneuvers needed to take the stronghold from the Japanese. After weeks on the beaches and in the adjacent jungle and fearful that a frontal attack will not succeed, General Cummings orders reconnaissance on a hazardous mission behind Japanese lines. The thirteen man platoon in its isolation and with almost unbearable hardships, demonstrates the worst and best in the men.

This is a profoundly moving depiction of men at war. The repetition of the reconnaissance trail enhances the men's fears and exhaustion and is deeply felt by the reader.

Tales of the South Pacific
James A. Michener (1907–1997)
New York: Macmillan, 1947

While reading *Tales*, the memorable songs from Rodgers and Hammerstein's hit musical, *South Pacific*, repeatedly run through one's mind. Many scenes, dialogue, song lyrics, and major characters are derived from vignettes in the book. For Broadway entertainment the tragedies and horrors of World War II in the Solomon Islands were played down or implied. But here are Lieutenant Cable, Liat and Bloody Mary, nurse Nellie Forbush, and French planter Emile de Beque set among the sometimes harsh beauties of the islands and the endless ocean. These ordinary men of all military ranks perform extraordinary feats to defeat the Japanese. Each chapter tells of the author's experiences and the people he encounters as he travels up and down the islands as an aide to Admiral Kester. And here are the well-defined characters both native and military: "big dealer" Seabee Luther Billis, the descendants of the mutineers from the bounty, the Remittance Man, among others, and the native tribes with their lives and traditions forever altered by the American servicemen. All this is played out against the background of the islands and the ocean, where some see the natural beauty, while others feel only the boredom and sameness of the surroundings. All feel the intense heat, suffer from the jungle rot and diseases, and think of their mortality and the ever-present Japanese. The men anticipate the long-awaited massive offensive against the entrenched Japanese on some to-be-named island.

Tales is a dramatic telling of the greatest adventure of its generation, a Pulitzer Prize winner for fiction in 1948, and a harbinger of many excellent books to come from the pen of James Michener.

The Fountainhead
Ayn Rand (1905–1982)
Indianapolis: Bobbs Merrill, 1943

Still a cult book in the 1990s on college campuses, it is among the top ten books read even when not assigned in courses. Two young men aspire to be architects: Peter Keating, traditional, classically trained, and with a modest talent, wishes to be famous and will use any means to reach his goal. Howard Roark, independent, freethinking, modernist with anti-establishment designs, and with exceptional talents, will not compromise and will support his ideas no matter what the cost. The exciting adventure moves logically and smoothly, and the descriptive writing is exceptional.

When taking the book to read in a public place, one should expect to be stopped and told, "That is the most wonderful book I ever read. I read it over again every two years." Its charm is obvious—if only real life were truly so black and white in its options. And if it were, would we really like it?

The world of Howard Roark and his love Dominique Francon is cold and impersonal where *none* of the usual emotions are felt or expressed. The creative hero Roark uses his mind well and becomes the fountainhead of all achievement, providing a moral basis for capitalism. He is in conflict with the world in every possible way, but at complete peace with himself. He will and must triumph over all others. Only the creative object is important. With Rand's philosophy of objectivism (there are nonfiction books by her and others on the subject), the common man is controlled, and through unity all will do and think alike. The world of Peter Keating is social and artificial, and living "this second-hand life," he is judged not by merit but by perceived success; but he is not happy because of everything lacking in his life. Two other important characters are Elsworth Toohey, a reprehensible, self-named critic who with his insane will for power, destroys others in order to control the world of the common man, and Gail Wynand, powerful owner and publisher of the *Banner,* who destroys others to keep control of the world he has created.

It is understandable why Ayn Rand's works are so universally praised or damned. Much of her philosophy is attractive, and although her prose is preachy and verbose, she tells a good story with interesting characters. To her supporters she is a visionary, to others an extremist.

The Human Comedy
William Saroyan (1908–1981)
New York: Harcourt Brace, 1943

Writing in a deceptively simple style, Saroyan relates the story of a second-generation immigrant American family, the Macauleys, of modest means in Ithaca in California's San Joaquin Valley during World War II. Father is no longer living. Mother is keeping her family together and raising her children with love and understanding. Marcus, the oldest, is in the army awaiting military assignment and Bess is in high school. Homer at fourteen is the central character with an after-school job as a telegraph messenger, and Ulysses at four is discovering his world with awe and wonderment. Homer faces both reality and illusion as he delivers his messages of death in wartime and love and money, bringing him in contact with naked and raw human emotions. He is entering adulthood, becoming a man in the midst of war, but in a world that appears safer, gentler, and more livable than our present age.

Primarily autobiographical, this story is presented through Homer's eyes, and he focuses on the people of the town and the natural surroundings of Ithaca where the pace of life is slower and the appreciation of simpler things is greater. Although easy to read for the day-to-day life story, there are multiple layers of emotion, faith, hope for the future, and unabashed patriotism. Be sure to pick up a copy with the delightful illustrations of Don Freman and revel in the lives of people you would like to see move in next door.

Shane
Jack Schaefer (1907–1991)
Boston: Houghton Mifflin, 1949

In 1889 the mysterious Shane rides into the Starrett family farm and rides out again. Is he the cause of the trouble or the avenging angel providentially in the right place at the right time to assist the good guys?

The inevitable western feud between farmers and ranchers, here set in Wyoming, is told by young Bob Starrett, who both fears and worships Shane. The vivid descriptions of the fist and gunfights, the cool detached Shane, the sympathetically drawn bad guys, the unexpressed emotions of Marian and Joe Starrett, and Bob who will not understand all that happens until he is grown. This western myth is beautifully written and no matter how well known with its inevitable conclusion can still be read with freshness and a sense of adventure.

Filmed by Hollywood, the color scenes taken in Jackson Hole are breathtaking. Jack Palance as the evil rancher-gunfighter and Alan Ladd as Shane will forever be identified with the characters. "He was the man who rode into our little valley out of the heart of the great glowing West and when his work was done rode back whence he had come and he was Shane."

What Makes Sammy Run?
Budd Schulberg, (1914–)
New York: Random House, 1941

The culture and ethos of 1930s Hollywood exemplified by antihero Sammy Glick, a self-promoting young man from New York's Lower East Side who rises to the top of the movie studio system. Sammy's story is told by a screenwriter he uses and discards along the way, an observer who nevertheless views that ascent with a measure of wry admiration even as he is never quite able to answer the novel's title question. Glick is both an explainable phenomenon and an enigma: his ambition is that of every ambitious immigrant, every new American who wants to fit into this sprawling society but never quite does, and who will never have enough money and power to feel secure and content.

Paralleling Sammy's story in interest is the novel's account of moviemaking in its formative years: Schulberg—later responsible for the screenplays of two of the most memorable films of the 1950s, *On the Waterfront* and *A Face in the Crowd*—has his Hollywood down cold, from roadster to mock Tudor mansion. An unexpectedly good read for its sociology and psychology as well as its fiction.

The Young Lions
Irwin Shaw (1913–1984)
New York: Random House, 1948

In the 1940s and 1950s, many authors tried to salvage meaning from the wreckage of war. While most books deal with strategy, generals, and major battles, *The Young Lions* tells the story of ordinary soldiers, two Americans and one German, during World War II. After a long and bloody war, the three men meet only in the novel's climactic scene. The book dramatizes the experiences and tragedy of both American and German participants in the war.

This is a riveting story, beautifully told by one of America's better writers. He deals with the scope and complexity of war and the randomness of death to those who are in it. A movie was subsequently made from the book.

A Tree Grows in Brooklyn
Betty Smith (1896–1972)
New York: Harper Brothers, 1943

With the background of the tenements in Brooklyn, housing mainly first and second-generation foreign immigrants in the teens, Francie and Neeley grow up in what today would be called a dysfunctional family. But what a wonderful family! Father is handsome, hard-drinking Johnny Nolan, a lovable Irishman; Mother Katie, pragmatically trying to keep her family clothed, fed, and educated; Aunt Sissy and her multiple husbands whom she calls all John; Aunt Evy and her ne'er-do-well uncle Willie; and Grandma Mary Rommely, among others. While the family is poor, the background is rich with vivid descriptions of shops and shopkeepers, street vendors, celebrations, and school days. All the sights, sounds, and smells of a bygone era! Francie, a loner, a daydreamer, and a resourceful child, finds her outlet in writing, and this book is primarily her story and her family's struggles. It would have been nice if just once the librarian had looked up and been kind to Francie, but even at the end of the book she cannot relate to the child who has been reaching out to her.

Reluctantly you leave Francie at seventeen wishing the book to continue but with a feeling of completion that does not require a sequel.

Strange Fruit
Lillian Smith (1897–1966)
New York: Reynal & Hitchcock, 1944

It is post World War I and a rather ordinary man, Tracy Deen, has returned to Maxwell, Georgia, from military service and renewed his teenage, ill-fated love affair with Nonnie Anderson. Tracy is white; Nonnie is college educated, black, and now pregnant. This "unholy liaison," flouting the ritual of segregation in a small Southern town of the 1920s, will affect all citizens regardless of social level or color. The whites will keep control, which has been disrupted by World War I and northern interference, and some of the less educated accept violence as the only method.

When a white man is shot, the killer must be black—almost any black will do, and justice must be immediate as practiced by "Judge Lynch." Smith's heroes and heroines are blacks who try to both accept and rise above their downtrodden status without offending the citizens and their employers on College Street. Preacher Dunwoodie, holding his revival meetings, is more concerned with bringing prominent white souls to God than with recognizing the underlying problems of Maxwell. Some of the town's leaders, who are respected by the blacks for their attitudes (which do not include future equality), recognize the unrest too late to stop the double tragedy.

This thought-provoking book, which was popular upon publication partially because of attempts to suppress it, has much to say to our times in spite of the advances in civil rights.

All the King's Men
Robert Penn Warren (1905–1989)
New York: Harcourt Brace, 1946

The lives of Jack Burden and "Cousin" Willie Stark, the Boss, are inextricably intertwined. Based loosely on the political life of Governor Huey Long of Louisiana. Jack tells the story of the rise and self-destruction of Stark—his frustrations, his corruption—while also telling about his own life and learning how to live it. This is a powerfully written story with strong messages of idealism and cynicism, of naiveté and duplicity, of American politics with its diverse personalities, and with the southern conviction that history is fate. Willie is a hero of the common man with a reformer's zeal, but he is a realist who learns to get his way through blackmail and payoffs. From southern backcountry, self-educated rube to booze-saturated vulgarian, he wields power and control while Burden becomes disillusioned and is witness to his destruction. Pairing this book with *The Last Hurrah* (Edwin O'Connor, 1956, see page 61), one can get a realization of mid-century American politics. A spellbinding tragedy of unrealized possibilities.

The movie, starring Broderick Crawford, won the Academy Award for Best Picture and Best Actor in 1949. The book won the Pulitzer Prize in 1947.

The Man Who Killed the Deer
Frank Waters (1902–1995)
Chicago: Sage Books, 1942

An eloquently composed narrative of Pueblo tradition and culture maintained on a United States reservation with agents determined to support "The American Way." In spite of poverty, the beauty of the land and the Indians' oneness with all living creatures and nature are poetically portrayed. Martiniano, the man who killed the deer, has been six years to the "away" school and is accepted by few Indians and none of the whites. He and his wife, Playing Flowers, are outcasts who partially reject both the old Indian ways and the white man's ways, thus being unable to live harmoniously within the shell of life. Martiniano hungers for a faith. But the plot is secondary to the described beauty of the landscape and the glimpses of Pueblo Indian life and tradition.

Although it is not uncommon for an author to have a significant though small national reputation with a strong regional following, Waters is one who deserves to be widely recognized and read. He has a thorough understanding of the American Southwest and Indian and Spanish-American values. He depicts such elusive themes as water, air, the Earth as a living entity, silence, spirits, and sacred lakes and mountains. Those in the Southwest will delight in their homeland and their heritage. Those outside will absorb a beautifully revealed lesson.

Another underrated writer, N. Scott Momaday, in his novel *House Made of Dawn* (1968) compels the reader to understand what it means to be Indian on the reservation and in the urban mainstream. Momaday's lyrical quality of expression foretells his future as a major poet of the American West.

Delta Wedding
Eudora Welty (1909– 2001)
New York: Harcourt Brace, 1946

Nothing can be more convoluted in its relationships, nor more supportive of its members, dead or alive, or more rejecting of outsiders, especially those who marry the pets of their family than an extended Southern family. Nine-year-old Laura McRaven, who has just lost her mother, is sent to the old Fairchild family delta plantation, Shellmound, in Mississippi. Her cousin Dabney is soon to be married (beneath her station) to the plantation overseer, but Laura cannot take part because of her mourning. The intricacies, harmonies, and discordance of family life are seen as the kin come from afar—the unmarried aunts, the great aunts, the remembered brother lost in the war, the not-so-welcome wife of the spoiled favorite brother, George. Laura is in awe of family and their ancestral homes but wins her place in the hierarchy. She idolizes the family unity of the Fairchilds regardless of age, and the novel sets forth the strengths and weaknesses of family ties.

In all, nothing much happens, but the exquisite descriptions, the captured speech of the region, and the lyric prose holds the reader. Most of the family members get to their own stories, all brought together by the wedding. This is a wistful remembrance of a somewhat romantic dreamworld of the landed gentry of the Old South in the 1920s.

The 1950s
Peace and Prosperity

The Korean War.

Color television is developed.

First inoculation of children against polio.

United States 42,000-mile interstate highway system started.

Montgomery, Alabama bus boycott.

The first commercial electronic digital computer, UNIVAC, is sold to the Census Bureau.

Elvis Presley cuts his first record.

The Soviet Union launches Sputnik. The United States follows with Explore I and Vanguard I.

The U.S. Supreme Court in Brown v. Board of Education, unanimously outlaws segregation by race in public schools.

Dr. Seuss publishes *The Cat in the Hat*.

The laser and the microchip are both patented.

Peanuts, Charles Schulz's comic strip, is first published; it will become the most widely syndicated in history.

A Death in the Family
James Agee (1909–1955)
Philadelphia: Lippincott, 1957

Life seems so uncomplicated in Knoxville, Tennessee, in the summer of 1915. It is the time before the Great War and the typical family spends its leisure going to the movies and taking long walks or an occasional automobile ride. This all changes very suddenly for the Follet family when father Jay is awakened in the middle of the night by a ringing telephone. It is his brother Ralph with bad news that their father is quite ill. Jay accepts his filial duty and sets off at dawn in the vintage Studebaker, leaving behind a worried wife, Mary, and their two children. When he reaches Grandfather Follet, it is only too apparent that once again Ralph has exaggerated and there was actually no need for Jay to have made this long trip.

Jay then begins the trip home. Mary is anxiously awaiting his arrival when the phone rings again late at night. This time it is a stranger who informs Mary that there has been an accident and it will be necessary for her to send a male family member to Brannick's blacksmith shop. The information is sketchy. How badly has he been hurt? Mary asks but receives no further information. So her brother Andrew volunteers to drive to Brannick's. Eventually he does contact his sister with the sad news that Jay has been killed in the accident, and speed appeared to be a factor.

This is mainly a story of how families bond together in a time of horrendous loss. Their sorrow is immeasurable. James Agee died two years before the publication of this book. It won a Pulitzer Prize in 1958.

Go Tell It on the Mountain
James Baldwin (1924–1987)
New York: Knopf, 1953

What would it feel like to be born black in Harlem in the 1930s? This is an in-depth study of the American Negro as the family struggles for survival and acceptance in a very perplexing city during the Depression. John is the eldest of four children of Gabriel and Elizabeth Grimes. He is aware from early childhood that his younger brother Royal is his father's favorite. The elder Grimes is a religiously obsessed preacher whose head is always raised upward toward the heavens instead of viewing his family on ground level. He believes that everything is a sin so a strict life is enforced on his children.

Elizabeth is the nurturing mother who stays home and tries to make life as pleasant as possible for her family. She has been saved by the preacher prior to the marriage, so her gratitude and dependence on him are overwhelming. Yet she harbors a past that makes her vulnerable to his criticism. Eventually one learns why John must deal with his father's partiality.

In flashbacks one learns of the racial struggles mother and father had to endure in the South before migrating to New York. The white supremacy credo below the Mason-Dixon Line made life unbearable. There is so much pain and struggle in the adults' former life. So it is clarified why Gabriel becomes such a religious fanatic, believing God directs him in every aspect of his life. You just want everything to change for them, for life to get easier and for all to live happily ever after. But it doesn't seem that this will ever happen. A famous book well worth reading.

Seize the Day
Saul Bellow (1915–)
New York: Viking, 1956

Almost any of Saul Bellow's novels could grace this page. In *Seize the Day*, middle-aged Tommy Wilhelm inadvertently learns about himself over the course of one day. He does not like what he finds out, nor does the reader. He looks slovenly; he squanders his money—a hapless comic figure. He is a loser. Recognizing this, his father rather coldheartedly refused to give him monetary assistance. Wilhelm is besieged from all quarters: no jobs, rent due, ex-wife threatening to sue over payment of child support, and his last dollars given to a charlatan to invest in the commodities market. His life in ruins, he passes a funeral. The tears he weeps for an unknown may suggest regeneration is possible.

But all is not tragedy as Bellow presents his characters at the Gloriana hotel, with its faded glamour, its attendants, and its aged residents, against a 1950s New York background. This is a moving story, both funny and profound, by a master of the writing craft.

Fahrenheit 451
Ray Bradbury (1920–)
New York: Ballantine, 1953

The classic novel on censorship and the best of science fiction; terrifying because it is plausible and the somewhat prophetic citizens of the United States have become so blasé and life is so humdrum that all they need is entertainment through visual images. Books are no longer read and are now banned, with firemen on emergency calls to burn books, the houses in which they are found, and, occasionally, residents. "Fahrenheit 451: the temperature at which book paper catches fire and burns." Montag, the fireman, realizes he is not happy with his life, and Clarisse, a strange teenager, disturbs him and makes him think. Life is cheap in the year 2000-plus and war against the haves by the have-nots is inevitable.

A particularly scary book, with its implications even greater today than in the 1950s as television and the Internet become the media of the day. In order to understand the lure and importance of all the other books described here, this novel should be read. All moral lessons aside, this is an exciting story for what will happen next, complete with vivid chase scenes with helicopters and the horrible death-dealing, mechanical Hound.

Breakfast at Tiffany's
Truman Capote (1924–1984)
New York: Day, 1958

Charming! Miss Holly Golightly sparkles and entertains in a New York easily recognizable today, although the 1950s scene is obvious in the alcohol and cigarettes and a somewhat unbelievable naiveté about the drug world. But all is wit and poignancy and Holly still knows nothing bad can ever happen to you at Tiffany's. Holly is a teenage hillbilly who married an older veterinarian in Texas and then moved to New York. She is known to many who have or have not read the book and will forever be associated with the actress Audrey Hepburn, who truly captured Capote's creation on the screen.

Truman Capote, a master of taut description and clever dialogue, was himself a character, best known for his short stories often appearing in *The New Yorker* and his true crime masterpiece, *In Cold Blood. Breakfast at Tiffany's* with its heroine will remain his best-known fictional work.

The Wapshot Chronicle
John Cheever (1912–1982)
New York: Harper Brothers, 1957

It has been said that John Cheever celebrates a world that is utterly ordinary—small-town New England with its eccentrics and faded illusions of gentility. The last word from Captain Leander, Mr. Wapshot, unsuccessful father to his sons, is all of the above: eccentric and ordinary, with faded illusions reflecting a sad wisdom and inadvertent humor. The setting is St.

Botolphs, a Massachusetts seaport, home of the Wapshot family. Father, practical mother, a matriarchal aunt who controls the money with strings attached and the two growing sons are in a long, steady decline. The book captures all the richness and absurdity of life with its characters encountering love, lust, and death. It is a joyful, tender and sad story and a delight to read.

By Love Possessed
James Gould Cozzens (1903–1978)
New York: Harcourt Brace, 1957

Before the recent spate of lawyer books and movies, some of the better written by John Grisham, there was Cozzens's *By Love Possessed*. The story of an honorable small-town attorney who learns the terrible secret of his longtime partners in the firm, it lacks the horror and flights of today but more than compensates with its well-developed characters, their conflicts of mind, and a well-told tale. Hailed as a masterpiece by many, it is limited to two days in the life of lawyer Arthur Winner, who admires reason, willpower, and judicious behavior, but all are tested and compromised as he makes ethical choices. He takes on the legal problem of his secretary's brother, Ralph, who is accused of rape and who jumps bail and disappears, leading the sister to commit suicide. Winner persuades the district attorney to defer charges by promising to use his influence in an upcoming judicial election.

Winner is forced to recognize his own vulnerability to these emotional pressures and the irrationality of most human demands—his safe world is crumbling. Also faced with the knowledge that his firm's senior partner has embezzled money and Winner's mentor has long known of the fraud, Winner must make the ultimate compromise with the man he believes himself to be. He becomes aware of his past self-justifications that he has submerged in a life dedicated to public service. A complicated story of the internal man told with compassion and in deceptively simple style.

Advise and Consent
Allen Drury (1918–)
Garden City: Doubleday, 1959

Washington's politics of power and ambition revealed. The power brokers, the outside influences, the lobbyists, the foreigners—all focused on one controversial presidential nominee, Robert A. Leffingwell for Secretary of State, when confirmed in the Senate. How will each senator vote and why? While reading the novel in 1959, one could easily recognize some barely disguised fictional characters, but this is not a distraction today. The book stands on its own merits as an outstanding depiction of the United States Senate in action, breaking and trading votes in its attempt to govern. You know each senator, who are like the men and women in office today. The international scene may change but the pressures remain the same—constituents, committee, responsibilities, presidential demands, foreign events, party allegiances and the press.

Here is a stormy political battleground with the details of the minds and motives of these statesmen, their public and private faces, their ambitions, vanities, hopes, and fears. This is a human story that scrutinizes man's weaknesses and nobility. The plodding arguments, political chicanery, moments of high excitement and tragedy, and talk, talk, talk lead to the final question: Will the Senate advise and consent to this nomination?

Invisible Man
Ralph Ellison (1914–1994)
New York: Random House, 1952

AND

Native Son
Richard Wright (1908–1960)
New York: Harper Brothers, 1940

These books show the two sides of invisibility, although Wright does not use the term in *Native Son*. Bigger lives in the ghetto of Chicago with little education and no job until a wealthy white benefactor hires him as a handyman and chauffeur for the family. Bringing the daughter home late at night after all the temptations of evil—drugs, alcohol, and sex—he accidentally kills her. He later kills his ghetto sweetheart with whom he constantly fights, is arrested for murder, and stands trial. He admits to himself that he is only fully alive and in control when he kills. He is defended by a Bolshevik attorney and is rightly convicted for all the wrong reasons. He is a victim of society, a nonexistent man ignored by the multitudes, and is executed. He forces the white man to see himself as the oppressor.

On the other hand, the nameless protagonist of *Invisible Man* lives and becomes truly invisible. Raised in poverty as a southern rural Negro, he receives the opportunity of an education and how to be an obeisant Negro in a northern white society. A brilliant student, he is literally "sold down the river" by his own people, and later co-opted and exploited by the communist movement. *Invisible Man* is a notable addition to twentieth century American literature, a classic expression of the black American existential and historical dilemma.

These are powerful books that helped change society, written by authors who came out of the Harlem renaissance. They changed a world and had their influence on the civil rights movement of the 1960s. Millions of words have been written about these titles and their influence, and editions have extensive introductory material because of their impact. Skip all that and create your own understandings based on today and the passage of time since the books were written. Read the introduction later if you wish.

The Blackboard Jungle
Evan Hunter (1926–)
New York: Simon & Schuster, 1954

Better known for his later 87th precinct detective stories written under the pseudonym of Ed McBain, Evan Hunter shocked readers with his first novel concerning conditions in certain New York public schools. Recent college graduate Rick Dadier secures his first teaching position at North Manual Trades High School. Because it is a vocational school he knows the kids will be tough, but he wants to teach and he has served a couple of years in the navy. He is happily married, a baby is on the way, and he idealistically confronts his new situation. His illusions are quickly shattered as he finds himself in a life-threatening situation, fighting against teenage gangsters after rescuing a fellow teacher from rape.

The book is a fast-paced action tale, eminently suited as the basis for the dramatic movie that followed. Strong characters are well drawn, and Hunter's skill in writing dialogue is well demonstrated here. The teachers are both sympathetic and inane, with incompetent administrators trying to overlook the horror in the schools. The kids see themselves as the losers they are and will continue to be as they strike out at the world. Escalate the horror with drugs and guns and the book is as relevant today as in the 1950s. Read it as a good action tale but think about its implications both now and in the future. This is an early fictional account that dramatizes what is still one of the top social problems in our country.

No Time for Sergeants
Mac Hyman (1923–1963)
New York: Random House, 1954

It's okay to laugh out loud. No matter how many variations have played on television, country bumpkin Will Stockdale and his sidekick Ben Whitledge's unintentional harassment of Sergeant King is still a hilarious story. Will and his father cannot prevent Uncle Sam from drafting Will. When Will pairs up with little Ben, who thinks he deserves a medal because his grandfather fought with Stonewall Jackson, this odd duo confounds the command of the United States military forces. Sergeant King becomes Will's nemesis determined to control the young soldier, but he is outsmarted at every turn.

Basic training was never meant to be like this. A wildly original series of humorous escapades ensues as Will accepts the honor of permanent latrine orderly and tries to please his sergeant by doing the best possible job. Although assigned to the elite air force, Will wishes to be infantry and will try to reach his goal through backwoods, commonsense, laugh-out-loud methods. These actions often make the tough, sometimes brutal, harassed Sergeant King a sympathetic character. The perfect actor chosen for Will's role, Andy Griffith, can be seen with an "aw shucks" grin on every written page. A book for a cloudy day!

From Here to Eternity
James Jones (1921–1977)
New York: Scribners, 1951

Probably one of the most accurate and intimate portrayals of life in the pre-World War II U.S. Army, with its chicanery, maneuvers, and the destruction of men who could or would not stay in the some ways very liberal lines set. It is written with contempt for the forces that waste human life and with compassion for men who find love, honor, and courage.

Most men are lifers, long-term complainers, but in truth in love with the army "bitch." They know of no more satisfying life, which they actually design. In many cases, although they are badly underpaid, the living is easy, especially in exotic Hawaii in Scofield Barracks. Although you do not know what role it will play with individual lives, you know the characters are facing the December 7, 1941 Japanese attack. Private (rank depending on the day) Robert E. Lee Prewitt is a thirty year career man in the profession, assigned to G Company. He will deny his talent as a bugler and fighter, defy "the bitch," and be destroyed. Others will be destroyed by their own paranoia, playing dangerously with sexual relations with officers' wives and prostitutes.

At its publication, readers were offended by the frank language and the men's preoccupation with sex. People remember the book but only one scene in the movie: sex on the beach with First Sergeant Milton Anthony (Burt Lancaster) and the Captain's wife (Deborah Kerr). This dominates the memory with good reason. Censors were presumably more restrictive in the 1950s, but the actual and implied movie actions created one of the hottest sexual liaisons in Hollywood history.

These men need war and will embrace it when it comes. They live by unspoken codes and with unutterable despair. A gritty, sweat-smelling, harsh, degrading, and uplifting life when men, women, and threat of war mix in an exotic background. It's a grabber!

Andersonville

MacKinlay Kantor (1904–1997)
Cleveland: World Publishing, 1955

Depressing and fascinating, emotionally powerful, depicting man's humanity to man. Andersonville Prison, where nearly thirteen thousand soldiers died, is synonymous with all the evils of prison camps and has now been designated as memorial to all the nation's prisoners of war. Kantor creates the Claffeys, a fictitious Confederate family who has lost three sons to the war. The prison for Yankees is built partly on their property. A man of courage, sensitivity, and pride, Ira Claffey and daughter Lucy cannot forget their losses but they can pity the prison inmates living under unbearable conditions. The Confederate officers are mixed: those who put their commissions on the line to report the truth and those like the vindictive General Winder, who is proud of killing more Yankees through overcrowding and lack of food, shelter, and medicines, than are being shot in the battle lines. Commander Henry Wirz, who through ignorance thinks he's doing the best he can, is the only Civil War soldier to be tried and hanged as a war criminal, a scapegoat to an outraged Northern public and a Southern martyr. You feel you personally know many of the prisoners, their former lives, their hopes and dreams, and you understand why they do or do not survive the deprivations and horrors of Andersonville.

A Pulitzer Prize winner, Kantor used information from available documents to create his true depiction of the prison life and his human portraits. His fictional local residents round out the picture. This was one of the most tragic episodes in American history, and the most glorious. Honored by Senator John McCain at the 1998 dedication of the National Prison of War Museum in Andersonville, Georgia were "all who were starved, dirty, sick, injured, suffering, dying—whose God-given dignity could not be destroyed by any human power, no matter how strong and malevolent."

On the Road
Jack Kerouac (1922–1969)
New York: Viking, 1957

Drugs, alcohol, sex, Asian philosophy, the open road in a speeding car, and petty theft all equal freedom. Such was the envied life of the Beats, portrayed in the sometimes lyrical prose of Jack Kerouac. The lifestyle contributed to a change in the American consciousness that led directly to the counterculture movement of the 1960s. From any perspective Dean Moriarty (Neal Cassady) is a user of anyone who befriends him, a loser in life with only Sal Paradise (read Kerouac) to stand by him, but he remains a cult figure today. Kerouac himself was a talent who never reached his full potential, and he is remembered primarily for his portrayal of Dean in *On the Road.* "A full five years to get through college. Most of the country's parents look at this sort of slacker ritual as the obligatory year of mush pitting, coffee drinking and Kerouac reading before graduation" (*Time,* June 9, 1997).

This book may be read to understand the Beat Generation of the 1950s and is still read by high school and college students who seek an understanding of self and feel close to Kerouac's portrait of alienation from the mainstream. Even the author's name has entered the language, e.g., "Before this, at 16, he had stolen a car and Kerouacked off to California" (*Time,* March 2, 1998). Kerouac's area of North Beach in San Francisco, still a lively hub at the City Lights Bookstore for neo-literary beatniks, is a major tourist attraction. In spite of vividly written portions where you can hear and feel the jazz music in the words, the speed of the car on the road, or the well-drawn characters, the book is overrated as a work of outstanding fiction.

A Separate Peace
John Knowles (1926–)
New York: Macmillan, 1959

The United States' participation in World War II overshadows the summer session at Devon School. The prep school boys will proceed as if nothing has really changed, as they argue, challenge each other, or do their pranks. It's another try to decide their role as they come of age for the draft. But one challenge between Gene, the lonely introverted intellectual (who narrates the story), and Phineas (Finny), the "Big Man on Campus," a handsome, taunting, daredevil athlete, will go awry and bring forth dark forces that hover over the tortured world of adolescence. What begins as a small incident among ordinary boys ends by evoking horrifying evil among all.

The characters are real, the setting is correct, and the tragedy in retrospect is inevitable. While each character fears an outward enemy—the Axis powers—the war fought on campus among themselves is far more tragic to the students. *A Separate Peace* is often considered an extension of Salinger's insight in *The Catcher in the Rye*.

Peyton Place
Grace Metalious, (1924–1964)
New York: Julian Messner, 1956

Surprise! This is a good story, well written with interesting characters. Greeted upon publication by a barrage of criticism about this "dirty" book, it is actually a highly moral tale with the good guys winning out in the end and the bad guys getting their just deserts. But all are equally the subjects of gossip. Metalious depicts the secrets and goings-on behind the closed doors of the people in a rigid, ingrown, small New England town (a typical American town?). As in most communities, there are past and present secrets, which eventually come to light, although there may be more than the average drunken binges, incest, tragic accidents and sudden death, abortion, rape, suicide, and murder with accompanying trial. Life should never be dull. And when reality is not enough, rumor and gossip make it better. Even the sins of past generations are dredged up to bedevil the present (late 1930s/early 1940s) residents.

The diverse people are presented with all the dimensions of their lives—their hopes and dreams, their evil and their goodness. They are realistic with recognizable personalities—they are human. The book in retrospect has been called a "modern literary soap opera with heart" and is interesting reading.

Lolita
Vladmir Nabokov (1899–1977)
New York: Putnam, 1958

Humbert Humbert is an acknowledged pervert particularly attracted to nymphets between the ages of nine and fourteen. His one true love is Lolita, who is twelve years old. In spite of its erotic subject matter, the book is neither lewd nor pornographic as some critics greeted it upon publication. Unlike current fiction, sexual scenes are alluded to, not graphically described; Lolita's gutter language is often decried but never explicitly written, and all bad guys are punished, including Humbert's tragedy of self-realization coming too late.

This novel is considered Nabokov's masterpiece and is historically important in the relaxation of censorship restrictions in American publishing in the 1950s. But primarily it is a parody of sexual perversions, commenting on American teenager Lolita's trashy mind; the trashy American movies; and the landscape with its cheap motels, junk food, tacky museums, and tourist traps where the couple travels. Even today the book is not what the first-time reader expects. It is also a satirical comedy of the confessional novel, the fictional diary, the romantic novel, as well as an adventure story in its own right. It has a hilarious grotesque scene of blood and gore and murder as Humbert repeatedly shoots his rival who keeps talking until he finally dies.

Its censorship history, its literary standing in academia (still read as an assignment), and its many published criticisms and analysis are heavyweights for a book to carry. The solemn breed of smut hounds will be shocked and disappointed because the book is intensely lyrical and extremely funny. Just read it and enjoy, and it's all right to laugh out loud.

The Last Hurrah
Edwin O'Connor (1918–1968)
Boston: Little Brown, 1956

The Irish and politics were synonymous in the first half of the twentieth century in large American cities, especially Boston, which is unnamed but the model for Mayor Frank Skeffington (suggested by Mayor James Michael Curley). Skeffington is loved by his Democratic followers and despised by all Yankee Republicans and Democratic reformers. Depending on the character's viewpoint, Skeffington is a lovable rogue, moving orator, generous to a fault, charming and witty, devious, guileful, manipulative, dissembling, evasive, underhanded, or ruthless. In his last campaign for mayor he gradually draws in his nephew, Adam Caulfied, who sees politics for the first time as practiced by an old-time mayor and his Irish tribal clan or machine. By election night the nephew has become as close as anyone could be to this complex man.

The novel is an inside picture of a political campaign in a changing world. Attending meetings, testimonial dinners, and wakes is no longer enough in the world of radio and newly emerging television. This is an entertaining, sentimental, and historical portrait of a political era told with the lilt of Irish voices and humor throughout.

Ten North Frederick
John O'Hara (1905–1970)
New York: Random House, 1955

The funeral of Joe Chapin provides the background for the biography of this wealthy, small-town Pennsylvania attorney, husband, father, and community participant whose personal and professional life is outwardly successful. But gradually the secrecy, deceit, and insensitivity are revealed. The main themes are introduced in the conversations at the funeral and burial, and then the development from family genealogy to the story of Joe's life and death occurs.

The story is fast-paced and dramatic, revealed through the author's gifts for replicating the speech and manners of people in a small Pennsylvania town and presenting accurate details of everyday twentieth century life. In spite of the unsympathetic characters, the reader wonders what will happen to each of them. There is Joe's wife, Edith, shrewd, hard, and possessive; his mistress Kate, who only wants to love him; his two children Joby and Ana whom he essentially destroys because their life choices offend his sense of respectability. In his political career, he rejects the party machinery managed by Mike Slattery and as a result is unsuccessful. His life crumbles, he turns to alcohol, and dies of an internal hemorrhage. A life revealed with its moral and human values and actions is as viable now as it was in the first half of the twentieth century.

The Light in the Forest
Conrad Richter (1890–1968)
New York: Knopf, 1953

A short, poignant novel of a young boy being forcibly returned by his Indian father to his biological white pioneer family. John Cameron Butler was captured by Indians as a small baby and adopted by an Indian family. He is raised as an Indian and emotionally feels himself to be the Indian true son. As a result of a treaty, at age fifteen he is returned to people he has learned to hate and to a life he neither understand nor likes.

The author tried not to write a historical novel but rather to create an authentic atmosphere of the life of early Americans moving into the wilderness to impose settlements on the frontier. He attempts to show how the first Americans felt toward this white conquest and the opposing attitudes of the early pioneers in the eastern part of the country. The dilemma of the human and heroic character who cannot exist totally in either the Indian or white culture is graphically portrayed but not resolved in an exciting adventure story. Often classified as a book for young adult readers, it can be read by adults as a concise, moving piece of fiction.

The Catcher in the Rye
J. D. Salinger (1919–)
Boston: Little Brown, 1951

Holden Caulfield, a precocious, misunderstood, mixed-up, alienated adolescent, is trying to survive his teens and become a man. He has become synonymous with the 1950s teenager expressing the phony (his favorite word) in middle-class America, which lead to the anti-establishment mood of the 1960s. Holden is both a rebel and a moralist, still known and understood by teens from all walks of life. The book and its reclusive author enjoy an almost cult like adoration in a time when major book promotion is the norm and a necessity for success.

Holden has again been expelled from a prep school and he heads to New York where he tries to become suave and cool with cigarettes, liquor, and dames. Everything depresses him with the one exception of "good old Phoebe," his ten-year-old sister, who understands him. The story is told in the first person. Everything goes wrong. Holden's sophistication disappears as he sees that everything is phony, and nothing cheers him up—in short, he is a troubled teenager.

Still readable (Holden Caulfied is in every generation) and still valid even though it reflects New York in the 1950s. It can also be a nostalgic piece if you can cut through Holden's unsatisfied thirst for goodness and perfection and his rebellious, confused passion to be an individual. It's also hard to believe how controversial the book was for many years after publication, and even today it is banned in some school systems.

Exodus
Leon Uris (1924–)
New York: Doubleday, 1958

This is a best-selling novel on the creation of Israel. An old adage reminds us that history repeats itself. However, in the case of Palestine, history never deviates.

Mark Parker and Kitty Fremont are Americans who meet in Cyprus right after World War II. At that time Great Britain has sequestered thousands of Holocaust victims who are trying to gain entry into Palestine. England fears too many Jews will incite the Arabs and threaten their own oil interests. These people are clinging to life in squalid conditions in Cyprus when Matt and Kitty visit the refugee camps. Mark uses his credentials as a journalist to gain sympathy for the cause, and Kitty's nursing training allows her to begin treating the sick and injured. Many of these survivors are children, and everyone wants to get out of Cyprus and put down roots in the promised land. Ultimately a ship, the *Exodus*, is sent to Cyprus and the refugees hastily board, uncertain if they will ever reach their desired destination. There is a confrontation with the British, but the ship does get to Palestine with minimal interruption.

These new settlers were responsible for taking a very barren, infertile land and irrigating it. By 1900 there were fifty thousand Jews residing in Palestine. In the 1930s, when thousands of Jews were desperately trying to leave Europe, the British government still restricted the number of visas issued, primarily not to alienate the Arabs. But after the war there were so many illegal immigrants as well as legal ones, and it seemed as though this overpopulation created more and more discord with the Arabs living in Palestine. The discord continues today.

The Man in the Gray Flannel Suit
Sloan Wilson (1920–)
New York: Simon & Schuster, 1955

Have things really changed that much? This is the post World War II generation who successfully struggled for upward mobility and spawned the generation who wanted it all. Thomas Rath, ex-army paratrooper and captain, and wife Betsy are looking for a better house in the suburbs, a new car, and savings to educate their three children. To do it Tom must risk all in a new venture in New York City, but must he also risk his own soul and become a yes-man to succeed? He wears the gray flannel suit uniform (a fairly universal figure in mid-twentieth- century America) and commutes daily to the city, frequently being called upon to stay late at night and be away from his family. Both Betsy and Tom question whether this is the life they dreamed about when they were first married. During the war their lives were complicated by Tom's war experiences when he killed seventeen men, had a brief love affair with an Italian woman, and fathered a child.

With the exception of the war experience and the change in uniform, the story could be set today, but Betsy would have to go to work outside the home. The central theme reflects the struggle for job security, and the desire for money and career versus family. An interesting book, readable with sympathetic characters and a message for our times.

The Caine Mutiny
Herman Wouk (1915–)
Garden City: Doubleday, 1951

The enduring image of career navy captain Philip Francis Queeg (Humphrey Bogart) rolling the small steel balls back and forth in his hand when under stress is one of those unforgettable moments in cinema and literature. Queeg the neurotic, the petty matinet, the revengeful paranoid, commands a bucket of bolts, a loose ship, the mine-sweeper *Caine*, past its prime when in service during World War II. Beside the incompetent Queeg, a half-comic, half-tragic figure, is the executive lieutenant officer, Maryk, an excellent but unsophisticated young career man who cannot cope with the developing situation, and lieutenant Tom Keefer, an embittered, witty intellectual who exacerbates the mounting tension on board ship. Step by inexorable step, the incidents lead to a takeover of the ship, a mutiny during a typhoon off the Philippines in December 1944. Maryk is court-martialed and his fate depends on the testimony of the story's narrator, Ensign Willie Keith.

Parallel to the events on the *Caine* is the maturity of this young Princeton boy who must serve his country in time of war. A "90-day won-der," he is disillusioned by his first assignment in the rundown *Caine* and he becomes involved in the catastrophic events. He is also trying to keep his former life on track back home, reconciling his long love affair with a Broadway nightclub singer, May Wynn, and his upper-class, disapproving mother. *The Caine Mutiny* is an intriguing modern sea yarn with the underlying question of discipline and command in a primarily civilian-based armed forces of a democratic society. A Pulitzer Prize winner.

The 1960s
Age of Idealism and Protest

The Cuban Missile Crisis occurs.

President Kennedy is assassinated; Jack Ruby kills accused gunman Lee Harvey Oswald.

Wide World of Sports premieres on ABC television.

First interplanetary space probes; Mariner II to Venus and Mariner IV flies by Mars.

Martin Luther King delivers his "I Have a Dream" speech. The Freedom Riders head to the South to test the Supreme Court ruling banning racial segregation on cross-country buses.

Biologist Rachel Carson writes *Silent Spring*.

The Surgeon General releases a report directly linking cigarette smoking to lung cancer and other diseases.

The war in Vietnam escalates; protests and resistance increase.

The Department of the Interior issues the first endangered species list.

The science fiction series *Star Trek* premieres on NBC.

Malcolm X, Martin Luther King, and Robert Kennedy are assassinated.

The United States puts the first men on the moon.

The Rector of Justin
Louis Auchincloss (1917–)
Boston: Houghton Mifflin, 1964

God or human? Sinner or saint? It all depends on who is speaking of Dr. Francis Prescott, the founder and longtime rector of Justin Martyr.

Brian Aspinwall, on his first job as an instructor of English at the Episcopal boys' boarding school, begins a journal. He falls under the spell of Prescott who in time becomes his mentor. The great rector now has his Boswell. Brian's observations are enhanced by the somewhat contradictory views of Horace Havistock, Prescott's oldest friend; Prescott's rebellious daughter Cordelia; David Griscam, a former student and trustee who wished to be Prescott's biographer; and Jules Griscam, David's son, who failed at Justin because of Dr. Prescott, among others. A profound analysis of a man's character, his personal crises and sins, his effect on others, his opinion of himself, his successes and his failures in both his public and private lives. Here also are the workings of famous private boys' school, which Prescott has created in his image, Justin Martyr.

This is the fascinating full-length portrait of a man's life from boyhood to his death at eighty-five, a character of reality and passion, a deeply religious man who played his role as God to many generations of schoolboys.

Little Big Man
Thomas Berger (1924–)
New York: Dial Press, 1964

The really true story of General George Custer and the Battle of the Little Big Horn told by the sole white survivor, Jack Crabb, also known by his Cheyenne relatives as Little Big Man. At over one hundred years of age, Crabb dictates the almost unbelievable adventures of his fifty years out west. He was a frontiersman, miner, buffalo hunter, soldier, mule skinner, gambler, every person you could ever expect to meet in the uncivilized Old West in the mid-nineteenth century, and he amazingly survived his travails.

His life crossed paths with notables: Chief Old Lodge Skins, Wild Bill Hickok, Wyatt Earp, Calamity Jane, and of course Custer. Crabb "by his own account was a participant in the prominent events of the most colorful quarter century on the American frontier. [He] was either the most neglected hero in the history of this country or a liar of insane proportions." His tale combines romance and realism, often correcting myths through his personal experience, and he tells of the relations of the soldiers, drifters, and settlers with the Indians—with mutual enmity and treachery on both sides, as he himself lives as both Cheyenne Indian and pioneer. He has lost a white wife to the Indians and an Indian wife to the whites. The book is a marvelous picturesque novel of the early West, outlandish and hilarious in its telling. A sequel *The Return of Little Big Man* (1999), continues the reminiscences of Jack Crabb and his fabulous adventures.

Red Sky at Morning
Richard Bradford (1932–)
Philadelphia: Lippincott, 1968

Mother and seventeen-year-old son move to their summer home at Sagrado in the mountains of New Mexico from Mobile, Alabama, when Father goes off to World War II. Josh Arnold revels in his new life with Mexicans, Anglos, and Indians while Mother, always the sheltered southern belle, turns to alcohol. With his two special friends, Steenie Stenopolus, the doctor's son, and Marcia Davidson, the rector's daughter, Josh will mature and learn about life and people from an alien background. He will be chased by Chango with a knife and become involved with the Cloyd sisters who will chase anyone with a car to drive. He will experience the peoples and superstitions of the high mountains with Sheriff Chamaco and be reminded of his southern past when the eternal guest (moocher, sponger) Kimbob Buel moves in.

Bradford has created rich characters from Negro servants to Anglo Mexicans with their unique dialects and speech, and has captured the teenage exchanges that pass for witty repartee. Against the harsh but beautiful background of the American Southwest, the author reveals the human comedy with happiness on the surface and tragic sadness underneath and the continued optimism of youth. This is a book that provokes laughter and tears and is simply an entertaining, well-written novel that is a joy to read.

Trout Fishing in America
Richard Brautigan (1935–1984)
New York: Dell, 1967

Reading Brautigan, a literary idol in the 1960s, was hip, but he now appears to be an acquired taste. Some of his best, more cohesive novels, *The Abortion* and *A Confederate General from Big Sur,* are difficult to find, but the innovative *Trout Fishing* added a new dimension to literature, is fun to read and the absurdities are laughable, a kinky book.

The book is written in short essays, sometimes only one paragraph long, describing Brautigan's life, adventures, and experiences mainly in California, in the 1950s and 1960s, as well as his earlier childhood. The author is a master of description with his anecdotal inventiveness, unusual similes, and colorful use of language. Here, his prose is close to poetry. He depicts a surrealist world of displaced young hippie types living with vague needs and irrelevant activities, while they eat, drink, get stoned, make love and occasionally fish. Each chapter is complete in itself with one little surprise leading to another in a stream-of-consciousness, mental meandering style. His early books were required reading for the Haight-Ashbury generation and Brautigan was called "the Last of the Beats" but his reputation faded in the 1970s.

His message seems to be that we will never really connect with each other. Today his work is enjoyable as a reflection of his era and for an evening's entertainment. Even now, where else do you find a book craftily ending with the word *mayonnaise*?

Mountain Man
Vardis Fisher (1895–1968)
New York: Morrow, 1965

Life is hard. No luxuries, no amenities, little or no human companionship. Death is commonplace—yours or those around you. Life is simply a struggle to survive by the strong and courageous, those with the skills and savvy of the natural world and the ability to live within themselves. That special breed of mountain men in the first half of the nineteenth century selected and preferred this way of life, this freedom. And through it all men like Sam Minard reveled in the majestic beauty and eloquent solitude around them.

Fisher has written one of the best depictions of a mountain man's adventurous life, exemplified by Sam, including his narrow escapes from hostile savages, his relationship with and respect for other Indian tribes, and his enduring love for an Indian woman. There is additional detail on his amazing physical endurance, his self-reliance, his occasional interaction with others of his kind, his visit to his family back east and his failure to adjust to that world. Even as Sam's American West is being changed by the increasing, destructive hordes of pioneers, he will remain as long as there is wilderness left. Here is the Old West without distortion, reality not myth, lyrically presented with fascinating charm, the rude, nomadic and hazardous way of life.

I Never Promised You a Rose Garden

Hannah Green (1932–)
New York: Holt, Rinehart and Winston, 1964

A dramatic recital of a young girl's madness. Deborah Alan, a "Jewish Princess" with all the material things one could desire and a pair of loving parents, is committed to an institution for the insane at age eighteen. Through vivid descriptions, the reader shares Deb's terrors, her imaginary world, which can ultimately destroy her, and the insanity of those around her, both inmates and a few staff. The gradual recovery of the control of the mind is as miraculous as the loss of control into schizophrenia is tragic.

Only someone who has been there can write so well about this debilitating mental disease. Being institutionalized by her parents, who accept all the social censure involved and receiving the help of Doctor Fried allow her to fight her illness and get well. The honorable doctor does not glorify reality; instead the only reality she offers is challenge and the ability to accept it or not. "Look here. I never promised you a rose garden."

The book immediately became a cult selection for collegians and later became popular with adult readers. Like *Catcher in the Rye*, a hit pop record in the 1970s borrowed its title. Originally having written under the pseudonym to protect her identity and her family, the real Hannah Green (Joanne Greenberg) was later revealed and has talked about her illness. A powerful book and deservedly still read.

Stranger in a Strange Land

Robert A. Heinlein (1907–1988)
New York: Putnam, 1961

Valentine Michael Smith, illegitimate son of astronauts of the first, lost colony sent to Mars, is raised by the "old ones" as a Martian. When he is brought to Earth as an adult by a later expedition, he must learn the culture and mores of a futuristic United States and adapt to its civilization.

His superhuman abilities, high intelligence, and insatiable need for knowledge cause him to "grok" everything he encounters and become water brothers to those Earthlings he trusts and admires. His teacher and constant companion is Gill Boardman, a nurse he meets in his first days on Earth. His disparagement of earth science, the hypocrisy and madness he sees, and his disgust at organized religions made the book highly controversial in its time. The second half of the story is the better known, as the gentle Mike tries to spread his goodness and superior knowledge through the establishment of a church based on love and communal sex (an act unknown to Martians) by teaching others to "grok." His unusual methods are gradually accepted by his friends and a few converts but misunderstood by most, leading to physical destruction and Smith's martyrdom.

Like American authors Brautigan and Vonnegut, among others, Heinlein was bred by the antiestablishment counterculture and was offensive to the mainstream. The work became one of the chief cult books of the 1960s and 1970s. Deservedly, the book now has a widespread audience beyond the cults and the field of science fiction. The reader, too, must "grok" Heinlein's humor and satire of our country, seen through alien eyes, as well as enjoy this disturbing adventure tale that still remains in the future.

Catch-22
Joseph Heller (1923–1999)
New York: Simon & Schuster, 1961

Before there was *MASH*, there was *Catch-22*. Different war, same hysterical lunacy, the military world turned upside down. Totally irrelevant black humor, and its antihero permit the reader to enjoy the comedy while realizing the absurdity of war. Even deaths become throwaway lines, and anyone seeking a discharge on the grounds of insanity is really sane enough to keep on fighting.

The term *catch 22* has entered the English language to imply a no-win situation and becomes more anti-hero relevant as time progresses. Even the antihero Captain John Yossarian has taken on a life all his own, exclusive of the book itself.

Although not truly a war novel, it grows out of World War II, is a strong protest against war (later used by Vietnam protesters), and is presented through grotesque, insane humor and satire. It contains one of the most horrifying depictions of the devastation of war, having the greater impact in a story mostly told through ludicrous events and scenes. Like other popular novels, it is difficult to separate the book from the movie, which captured the essence of Heller's book. Laugh, cry, and feel the impact hit you like the proverbial ton of bricks.

Up the Down Staircase
Bel Kaufman (1911–)
Englewood Cliffs: Prentice Hall, 1965

Teachers are paid to teach, administrators are paid to administrate, but somehow they don't always work together. Anyone who has ever been in a public school classroom can laugh at these directives to teachers while they still feel the frustration in trying to comply when they should be giving attention to their students. And an inexperienced new teacher like Sylvia Barrett sometimes needs an old hand to translate the memos!

In *Staircase* a dedicated teacher's ideals challenge the educational bureaucracy—the trivia in multiple copies, which actually contributes to the lack of communication. But it comes down to real people and the love that can be generated between student and teacher. Good teachers mean good education. The book allows the characters to speak in their own words through memos, letters, directives from the administrators, comment by students in a suggestion box, and papers from desk drawers and waste baskets. The children portrayed are characters asking for more than just the teaching of English, and a new teacher begins to hear what they are saying. (Even the title becomes a part of the language, applied to the chaos of modern society.)

Although fiction, Kaufman's book portrays the real world of a big-city high school that has changed since the 1960s but not necessarily for the better. The inadequate buildings, overcrowded classrooms, heavy teaching loads, inane directives, and the problems of youth have increased. But all is not lost. Reading the book still reveals the joy of teaching beneath the stress and humor. "Hi, teach! Hi, pupe!"

One Flew over the Cuckoo's Nest
Ken Kesey (1935–)
New York: Viking, 1962

Some of the more unusual characters in fiction. Miss Ratched, or Big Nurse, controls the male ward of a mental hospital through fear and intimidation until the anti-hero, Randall Patrick McMurphy, personable con man, arrives and says and does what everyone else can only think about. He swaggers in and takes over, rallying the other patients and challenging the dictatorship of Big Nurse.

And all this is told by one who is admittedly mentally ill but who sees the ensuing conflict, and also describes strange goings-on that could only be exaggeration based on reality developed in a sick mind. Definitely a book of the counter culture 1960s rebelling against the controlling forces of society, with its sometimes misguided idealism, and social change. Kesey vividly presents descriptions of patients and their environs and draws the reader into the actions and surroundings. McMurphy's defiance, which starts as a game, develops into a grim struggle, with the inmates as pawns. McMurphy has an indomitable will and for the most part the backing of the men, who are gaining strength and belief in themselves.

As a result of McMurphy, they may be able to regain the outside world, such as the narrator, Chief Bromden. Big Nurse has the power of full authority and she will win, using all the weapons at hand. Her ultimate choice will turn the contest to disaster. A book celebrating life, uplifting as man conquers fear, and tragic as men destroy one another.

To Kill a Mockingbird
Harper Lee (1926–)
Philadelphia: Lippincott, 1960

A warm, beautiful story of a young girl, her older brother, and growing up in a small southern town, complete with all the myriad eccentrics found in such a setting.

Jean Louise (Scout) experiences the delights of childhood but must gradually come to grips with the prejudice and violence that are acceptable against the black population of the town. Atticus Finch (played in Hollywood by Gregory Peck) is a loving single-parent father who is sometimes overwhelmed by his life trials but has a strong belief in racial justice, which he lives by, and stands as an example for his children. He takes the unpopular stand as a lawyer in defending the unjust conviction of a black man accused of raping a white woman and tries to protect his children from the woman's poor, white father bent on the destruction of Finch's family. Because the somber tale is seen through the eyes of a small child, it takes on a more terrifying and dramatic dimension.

Although a first and only novel, *Mockingbird* won the Pulitzer Prize in 1961. It is a moving book that puts the racial tensions of the time in perspective as well as treating the children's unintentional cruelty in dealing with a mentally disabled neighbor they fear. Although it tells a bleak story, it has its moments of good humor, warm relationships, and a clever climax to resolve the crisis. A book to be read more than once.

The Fixer
Bernard Malamud (1914–1986)
New York: Farrar, Straus and Giroux, 1966

A sad, depressing, dramatic book. The Fixer, Jewish by birth but a nonpracticing religionist, is arrested for the murder of a Russian child. He, Yakov Bok, is cited as an example of Jewish bloodlust and criminality. Although innocent and not indicted, he is held in prison under gradually worsening conditions while his jailers hope that he will confess so as to serve the state and justify the persecution of Jews as a policy. He is kept in solitary and can see no hope of a trial or release. If the case were tried, his conviction or acquittal would cause a pogrom against the Russian Jews. Gradually he understands his Jewishness and feels a sense of belonging as a victim of persecution. Regardless of the severity of his treatment, he steadfastly maintains his innocence and believes freedom is due him. He insists on a trial. It is a time of political unrest in Russia (Kiev, 1911) and the Jews are seen as instigators and conspirators by both the reactionaries and the government of the tsar, who would retract the basic freedoms gained after the revolution of 1905.

Yakov, not knowing it at first, is part of history—the part where a Jew carried on his back "a condition of servitude, diminished opportunity, vulnerability." No Jew was innocent in a corrupt state. The novel deals with anti-Semitism and general human injustice. The story is based on the historical case of Mendell Beliss who worked for fifteen years in a Kiev brickyard before he was charged with the ritual murder of a Christian boy. Beliss was acquitted in a trial important in the history of Jewish persecution. A Pulitzer Prize winner.

The Group
Mary McCarthy (1912–1989)
New York: Harcourt, Brace & World, 1963

It all begins and ends with Kay, the one outsider in the group. The seven girls are from privileged families, newly graduated from Vassar College (class of 1933), and ready to set the working world on fire with their brilliance and education. They are assembled with their hats and gloves and fashionable clothes for their unpredictable classmate Kay's surprise wedding.

While not planning to deliberately flaunt traditional social conventions, each young woman expects to enter some aspect of professional work, unlike their conservative, society-matron mothers. Their energy and optimism are infectious as they gossip, plan, and plot. They will not all keep in close contact, although their lives will intertwine and they will come together at Kay's funeral. In the intervening seven years they have married, had babies, or become professional women, but generally things have not turned out as they dreamed. The members of the group have sought without much success to build satisfying lives for themselves in a pre-women's lib, male-dominated society. Each in her own way has struggled against social restrictions and sexual expectations, which have pervaded most of their lives.

The novel is an interesting biographical study of eight unique individuals and a chronicle of their generation.

Tropic of Cancer
Henry Miller (1891–1980)
New York: Grove, 1961

This novel, in the form of a personal narrative, is a monologue that is heavily anecdotal and philosophical. This story of a writer in Paris in the 1920s and 1930s deals with the author's poverty, hunger, and complete physical and spiritual degradation. A very angry and sometimes humorous book, it tells the story of a poor artist, including his seedy life and sexual experiences, which the author believes are good when animated by love.

Originally published in Paris in 1934, the book was banned in the United States for thirty years on grounds of obscenity. The first American edition was published in 1961 and became a best-seller. Some readers believe the book is dated, but others consider it Miller's best work, with some of the better comic scenes of modern literature.

Them
Joyce Carol Oates (1938–)
New York: Vanguard, 1969

This is a good example of how we can create our own misery in life. After her brother Brock murders her boyfriend in her bed, Loretta Botsford literally marries the first man who comes along. This allows her to escape her miserable home life and begin building her own dysfunctional family. Howard Wendall is a policeman, and together he and Loretta embark on holy matrimony. Two children are born rather quickly. Howard loses his job after a political investigation reveals his involvement in illegal activities. The newlyweds join forces with Howard's elderly parents, move to a farm in the Midwest, and remain there for several years. With the advent of the Second World War, Howard joins the service just as Loretta realizes she is pregnant for the third time. When she receives a letter from an old friend, Loretta decides to join her in Detroit rather than remain isolated on the farm.

Howard returns to Detroit when the war ends with no ambition and a severe drinking problem. His bouts with alcohol greatly affect the children. Jules finds his release on the street, and although he has a few brushes with the law, manages to stay out of any serious trouble. Maureen, meanwhile, prefers the solitude of the town library where the peace and quiet are a contrast to the constant fighting between her parents. Betty prefers to hang around the house. It is obvious these children are emotionally damaged by the lack of nurturing in their childhood. One hopes they will attain happiness in life, but it doesn't look promising.

The Moviegoer
Walker Percy (1916–1990)
New York: Ivy Books, 1961

Binx Bolling is a small-time stockbroker who lives quietly in a New Orleans suburb and enjoys movies and affairs with his secretaries. His well-ordered life is disturbed by his aunt's insistence that he talk to his stepcousin Kate, who is rather charmingly mentally unbalanced and under treatment for her suicidal tendencies.

In time, Binx realizes his love for Kate, but she is too self-absorbed to work with him on their problems. Binx's half brother Lonnie is the catalyst that brings the couple together and helps set Binx on his way to a more ambitious life with meaning. Set in New Orleans during Mardi Gras, Percy's novel captures the flavor of the city and its inhabitants. He writes a book of despair, which is both witty, and at times hilarious. This is a rather strange though beautiful story, with much implied rather than stated.

Ship of Fools
Katherine Anne Porter (1890–1980)
Boston: Little Brown, 1962

The storms of war that were to envelop Europe and most of the world in World War II are foretold in the attitudes and interactions of the passengers on the German ship *Vera*. Although the voyage is depicted as dull, the passengers' inner lives are revealed—their fears, loves, hates, and accepted (but horrifying) beliefs. Being locked into contact on shipboard during twenty-seven days in 1931, the worst side of each person is gradually exposed. This is a novel on a grand scale reflecting the variety of life. Many of the passengers, like the Captain and the ship's doctor, are Germans who, although flawed themselves, revile their fellow passengers who are Jewish, Spanish, American or Cuban and the more than eight hundred unfortunates in steerage being deported to Spain after the crash of the sugar market in Cuba. The story is crafted from the meeting and mingling of these various personalities and a drama of good and evil. There are episodes of personal unkindness and cruelty, stubborn prejudices of the "ruling race of the world" who are against non-Nordic races, and the reciprocal and destructive hatred between Jew and Christian—all played out against a world on the edge of catastrophe with people blind to the imminent disaster. The "Ship of Fools" is the ship of humanity.

Although somewhat slow reading to a present audience that is accustomed to more action and not sailing by ship as transportation, the story holds one's interest and creates an emotional impact through its statements such as expressed by the Captain: "That was his true world, of unquestioned authority, clearly defined caste and carefully graded privilege. He knew well what human trash his ship carried. There was only one course to take: *they must be put down with fire and sword.*"

True Grit
Charles Portis (1933–)
New York: Simon & Schuster, 1968

Read some of the magnificent Westerns (*The Virginian, Riders of the Purple Sage,* and *Shane*) and follow it up by this irreverent take off on all things held holy in western fiction.

The law is represented by over-the-hill, alcoholic, "shoot the bad guys dead," not too bright, one-eyed Rooster Cogburn; an equally dense bounty hunter, a gunslinger from Texas; and a most improbable heroine, smart-mouthed, bossy, demanding, conniving fourteen year old Mattie Ross, bent on avenging her father's death. The supporting cast is here also in a skewed fashion: the traditional boardinghouse and its motherly manager, the slightly shady livery owner who thinks he can cheat a child, and a frontier lawyer from back home who supports Mattie and would feel right at home in contemporary litigation. Of course, the outlaws are inept and cannot hope to outsmart Mattie. Even the grand vistas of the West are suspect in Fort Smith, Arkansas, and Indian Territory.

Mattie controls the adults with her wits and her indestructible vitality and harshness which will amuse, touch, and sometimes horrify the reader. This is an eccentric, witty, original view of the icons of the Old West. And the greatest traditional Hollywood western movie hero of them all, John Wayne, played Rooster to perfection.

The Chosen
Chaim Potok (1929–)
New York: Simon & Schuster, 1967

A hard fought, highly competitive baseball game changes the lives of two boys and their fathers. Danny Saunders of the Hasidic Jews is destined by inheritance to be the unwilling leader of his sect, while Rueven Malter wishes to be a rabbi. Set within a few blocks in Williamsburg in Brooklyn, the teenage boys are miles apart in tradition because of their sects. The story evolves around the development of their special friendship and their vastly different relationships with their fathers. Their beliefs, the intensive study and interpretation of the Talmud and their religious traditions play major roles in the lives of these two brilliant boys as they grow from boyhood to manhood, leaving the yeshiva for college.

The author brings alive the period at the end of World War II with the revelations of the Holocaust and disagreements over the development of the state of Israel. This beautifully written novel of Jewish life relates the universal themes of pathos, love, and compassion.

The Godfather
Mario Puzo (1920–1999)
New York: Putnam, 1969

The Godfather is claimed to be the best-selling novel in publishing history. This is the story of the powerful mafia Corleone family with its don, the Godfather (forever identified with movie actor Marlon Brando), who controls with favors, friendship, wisdom, and horrific violence. He establishes himself as the powerful Don and peace reigns until he refuses to take the family into the newly developing drug traffic. The Don is shot, the Corleones retaliate, and the Five Families War of 1946 begins.

Sonny, the oldest son, leads the troops until he is killed and the old, semi-recovered Don takes over, calling a peace conference to buy time to rebuild and coining a new phrase, *Costra Nostra*. But the family may regain its power, influence, and price, only with a new don, the unwilling youngest son, Michael, a college-educated war hero, smart and brutal. The Corleone family chooses to live outside the accepted laws and mores of the mainstream society but have a strict standard of ethics for themselves and their workers, that is adopted from their Sicilian homeland. In spite of the violence and the illegal activities, the Corleones are not portrayed as ruthless mobsters and the reader cares about the family and their fates.

The book portrays the struggle that all immigrants face: the need for respect, for security, for a sense of belonging. The Don may be a mob boss, but he is a father also who wants to see his children achieve more than he has been able to.

Portnoy's Complaint
Philip Roth (1933–)
New York: Random House, 1969

This is the story of Alexander Portnoy, the bright but driven son of Sophie, a textbook "Jewish mother." All of Mama's energy is directed to constructing a perfect boy. She is with him every step of his childhood, smothering him, demanding to know his every thought and every move.

Father Jack is a life insurance salesman back in the days when premiums were collected door-to-door. He is out of the house a lot, but when he does return, it's usually to a bedlam he manages to intellectualize. Finally Alex grows up and eagerly leaves his Jewish mother behind. His visits home become less frequent, and Sophie inevitably uses their little time together to make him feel guilty for his lack of attention. And at this she excels. In her own mind, Sophie's biggest flaw is the fact that she is just *too good*.

Alex's relationships with women are as would be expected-very pathetic. His choices are generally women he finds sexually attractive but with very little else to attract him. Ironically he gives them strange nicknames like "Monkey" or "Pumpkin" and the affairs are short-lived. Perhaps he subconsciously believes he just might marry his mother. But since childhood Alex has been so in love with his own body—why would he ever need a mate?

The Agony and the Ecstasy
Irving Stone (1903–1989)
New York: Doubleday, 1961

This is a story of perhaps the greatest artist in history and his patrons. Michelangelo was born in 1475 in Florence, Italy, the second oldest of five boys. At thirteen he is apprenticed as a sculptor and eventually is invited into the palace of Lorenzo de' Medici to create engravings. Given a small salary and a studio to set up his art supplies, he quickly becomes close to the Medicis.

In the fifteenth and sixteenth centuries the papacy ruled Italy. Michelangelo's immense talents are sought out in Rome by the papacy, and he spends much of his time commuting between Rome and Florence. Where one pope would praise his work, the next might refuse to fund his projects or take a long time to properly compensate him for the work he completed for the Church. Painting the ceiling of the Sistine Chapel takes years and is a terrible burden on his body.

Pope Julius II is reigning when the chapel work is completed on November 1, 1512, after four years. Then Julius is succeeded by Leo X. Whereas Julius spent a fortune on war, Pope Leo is determined to spend his funds on art. Next in line is Pope Adrian, who demands that Michelangelo return money for the tombs he started with Julius's reign. Finally, when Michelangelo is in his early eighties, Pope Paul IV, a rigid fanatic, comes into power. He demands that the *Last Judgment* fresco be whitewashed since some of the characters are nude. A public outcry overturns this ultimatum eventually to the benefit of the world.

This is biographical fiction; Irving Stone spent years in libraries doing research on this great artist. As much as this book is about Michelangelo, it is also about the sanctimoniousness of an organized religion.

The Confessions of Nat Turner
William Styron (1925–)
New York: Random House, 1967

In August 1831 the first recorded revolt by a band of American Negroes took place in Virginia. There were over sixty slaves involved and seventeen survived to be hanged, including Nat Turner, the leader. This is his narration. It is less a historical novel than a meditation on history.

Nat's story begins when he is in jail waiting to die after the insurrection, and it quickly regresses through his tragic life. His mother is a cook in a Virginia household, so he did have a few minor benefits. When he was very young, he stole a book from the main house. Instead of being punished, his sympathetic master taught Nat how to read. After that, the white family was fond of telling their neighbors how intelligent this child is. Perhaps they also felt it would increase his value if he were to be placed on the auction block. But kindness, ever so fleeting, was rare for slaves. Nat is taught carpentry so he doesn't have to work the fields, and his life, as he views it, is not as horrific as it is for some of his black brothers and sisters. Still, he yearns constantly for freedom. After a few years, the owner explains to Nat that the Samuel family is moving to Mississippi for economic reasons and is going to sell off most of their slaves. Nat is to be sent to a preacher where he will live according to the law of God and be prepared to go out into the world. Eventually Nat will be sent to Richmond and given his freedom. He rejoices when he hears this news.

So, at the age of twenty one, Nat arrives at the squalid home of the Reverend Eppe, a Baptist preacher. It is the sentiment of Mr. Samuel that the "Man of God" will treat Nat kindly. But he is farmed out to everyone in the neighborhood, overworked, and given too little food. The ultimate betrayal occurs when Eppe sells him at auction to a cruel master, despite his promise to Samuel. His new owner, Thomas Moore, beats him with a bullwhip after he asks for food, and life becomes unbearable. Embittered and driven by supernatural visions, Turner becomes the leader of a small band of other Southampton slaves, who plan a mutiny on a day when a revival meeting is being held in the town. The slaves manage to arm themselves with a quantity of guns and ammunition. As the townspeople leave for the revival, the carnage begins. Many white men and women are murdered. The rebellion is put down with great speed and brutality. Those captured, including Turner, are hanged as a message to other slaves. A powerful and moving book that won the Pulitzer Prize in 1968.

Rabbit, Run
John Updike (1932–)
New York: Knopf, 1960

Spontaneously and unplanned, Harry Rabbit Angstrom, former high school basketball star, now twenty-six, runs away from his life; his parents; his in-laws, his son; especially his pregnant, nearly alcoholic, stupid wife; and his job as a salesman for the household gadget Magipeel. Rabbit runs into the small town of Brewer, adjacent to his hometown of Mt. Judge, and into the arms of a prostitute, Ruth, who becomes his mistress. Updike writes some of the best, clearly descriptive (but nonclinical) sex scenes between two consenting adults.

Soon everyone knows where Rabbit is and what he is doing. In a time of crisis, Rabbit runs back to his wife. It does not last and Rabbit again runs away from his wife, with tragic consequences. Ruth is now his pregnant mistress and Rabbit runs from reality—to what he doesn't know. He is an irresponsible, hollow, narcissistic, philandering, self-contemptuous, self-pitying man in what is often seen as a hollow generation. He is sensitive enough to feel guilt but cannot face his obligations. Rabbit will run through several future novels as he ages, all in Updike's effortless prose style written in the present tense.

Slaughterhouse-Five
Kurt Vonnegut, Jr. (1922–)
New York: Delacorte, 1969

An unconventional novel organized as a collection of impressions that focuses primarily on the horror and absurdity of war and man's helplessness in that situation. Billy Pilgrim, in the U.S. Army, gets lost behind German lines during the Battle of the Bulge, is captured, and is systematically reduced to a vegetable. In this state he witnesses the infamous bombing of Dresden in which 130,000 people were killed. Billy must live with this experience for the rest of his life, goes quietly mad, and escapes into the fourth dimension. Here is Vonnegut at his best—facing the horrors of life and living in the fantastical dream-world when life becomes too gruesome. With the good dream associated with the bad dream, life becomes almost bearable.

The words create images or symbols that, taken all at once, envision the real world.

Science fiction addresses the meaningless of life seen in the war, and man survives through the creation of harmless lies written in short chapters. A masterful story of reality and fantasy for adults, that became part of the cult literature of the 1960s anti-war movement, but still readabile and valid today. Or, as Vonnegut added to his title page in a later edition: "A fourth generation German American now living in easy circumstances on Cape Cod and smoking too much who, as an American infantry scout hors de combat, as a prisoner of war witnessed the fire bombing of Dresden, Germany, 'The Florence of the Elbe,' a long time ago, and survived to tell the tale. This is a novel somewhat in the telegraphic, schizophrenic manner of tales of the Planet Tralfamadore where the flying saucers come from Peace." So it goes!

The 1970s
A Changing America

The United States restores relations with China; Nixon visits China.

Roe v. Wade.

OPEC increases oil prices.

Three Mile Island accident.

Monday Night Football debuts on ABC.

The Vietnam War ends.

The world's first commercial video game, Pong, is introduced.

The Watergate scandal forces the resignation of President Richard M. Nixon.

The satiric comedy show *Saturday Night Live* premieres.

Hammerin' Hank Aaron breaks Babe Ruth's record with his 715th home run.

Iranian revolutionaries storm the U.S. embassy in Tehran, holding 52 Americans hostage for 444 days.

Environmentalists celebrate the first Earth Day.

The Monkey Wrench Gang
Edward Abbey (1927–1989)
Philadelphia: Lippincott, 1975

A wildly comedic, fantastic, almost tragic, but quite serious attack on the manmade objects that desecrate the desert landscape of Utah and Arizona.

George Washington Hayduke is home from the unpopular Vietnam War to refresh his soul in the desert paradise he has dreamed about. His fury at the destruction of the Colorado River leads to his conversion into a firebrand environmental radical who plans retaliation. He joins forces with three like thinkers: Seldom Seen Smith, backcountry guide and jock Mormon, O.C. Sarvis, surgeon, and his assistant and companion Annie Abbzug, formerly of the Bronx. They form an unlikely quartet—the Monkey Wrench gang. Using chain saws on billboards, disabling bulldozers and heavy road equipment, and destroying bridges, they dream of the "Big Kill—the Glen Canyon Dam."

As they wreak their havoc, they face the forces of Bishop Love and the San Juan County Search and Rescue team, later combined with the Department of Public Safety State of Utah. The sheriffs of three counties among others, create some of the best car chases in literature with jeeps, trucks, off the road vehicles and helicopters along the almost nonexistent roads of the backcountry. There is biting, crude repartee and spectacular descriptions of the land as the environmental anarchy continues. A modern fairy tale that made Abbey (Cactus Ed) a cult hero.

Richard Bradford, author of *Red Sky at Morning*, summed it up best on the book's dust jacket: "Destroying eyesores is simply another way of creating beauty, and Edward Abbey's dedicated crew are masters of this particular Renaissance of course. What the *Monkey Wrench Gang* does is outrageous, un-American, and inimical to the sacred concept of property, and I thoroughly condemn them. If unchecked, they may even start dumping tea in Boston harbor."

Shogun
James Clavell (1924–1994)
New York: Athenaeum, 1975

"Shogun" was the title of military rulers of from the twelfth to the nineteenth centuries who governed Japan. This is the story of an English navigator, Blackthorne, who, when shipwrecked off the coast of feudal Japan, becomes a pawn in a deadly struggle between the warlord, Torango, and the Emperor. Torango is driven to become supreme military dictator and is prepared to kill his rivals. The Portuguese have a monopoly on trade with Japan as well as in Christian religious matters. So there are conflicts between Protestant England and Catholic Portugal. There is also a love story between Blackthorne and a Japanese lady, Mariko.

The book shows the impact of the West on seventeenth century Japan and leads to an understanding of Japanese history. It was made into a popular TV miniseries and movie starring Richard Chamberlain.

The Great Santini
Pat Conroy (1945–)
Boston: Houghton Mifflin, 1976

Lieutenant Colonel Bull Meecham is the Great Santini. A United States Marine, fighter pilot, and war hero, the Corps and flying are the most important things in life. He is the epitome of the tough marine officer, a disciplinarian both at home and on base. The Catholic Church and family life come second. At times funny and witty, at times violent and shocking, such as when Bull beats his wife and children while trying to shape the children's lives. His sons have to be marine pilots, his daughter wives of marines.

This absolute ruler of his family does not tolerate rebellion or even a difference of opinion. Conroy (Ben) tries to present his father in the best possible light, but the truth presents the other side. As a result there is a mixture of hate and fear as well as unacknowledged love in the son. Nothing less than perfection is considered acceptable. What matters is winning regardless of the means. Ben is determined to be himself (he is a natural-born athlete, pleasing to his father), whatever that will be, but he must stand up to his father and fight back. Mother Lillian, a beautiful southern belle, usually knows how to manipulate her husband, and with her cool head and core of velvet steel, helps Ben and her other three children work through their dealings with their father. The other destructive influences on the kids are the constant rootlessness and being disconnected from the rest of society, true of all military families. Fortunately, Conroy also shows his humor, an integral part of his own nature shown in later books.

Hard-edged, disorienting, sometimes ugly, sad, and "laugh-out-loud" humorous, this autobiographical book is wonderfully written by Conroy, who brings his characters to life. All of his books can be recommended.

I Heard the Owl Call My Name
Margaret Craven (1901–1980)
Garden City: Doubleday, 1973

A young priest, Mark, unaware that he is dying, is sent by his bishop into the harsh seacoast lands of British Columbia to the parish of the Kwakiut Indians, who earn their livelihood from the sea and the forest. With patience, faith, and understanding, Mark will minister to the people, learn their ways, earn their respect and ultimately their love. Among these Indians, whose culture is gradually being destroyed by the civilization around them, he will learn much about himself as well. He becomes part of the village and its culture. He will watch the loss of the young people as they go to school on the mainland, some to be effectively absorbed, some not, but never to return. He will see the tragic results of the introduction of alcohol to the village of Kingcome.

But Mark will learn to appreciate the belief of the Indians that the village encompasses the myths, the river, the salmon, the bluejay, the grizzly, and the owl who calls the name of the man who is going to die. Although sad, the book's lyrical telling and message of faith are uplifting to the reader.

Deliverance
James Dickey (1923–1997)
Boston: Houghton Mifflin, 1970

What a master of description! You can see and feel every toehold and fingerhold as Ed Centry climbs the cliff from the river for his own and his companions' survival. Four average suburban American men challenge an uncharted river in Georgia and face violent adventure and inner discovery. What is meant to be a break in their daily routine, a chance for adventure with few risks and the last time to see a beautiful river valley before the river is damned, turns into a nightmare. Their leader, a champion at most sports and an enthusiastic outdoorsman, wishes to pit man against nature.

When two of the men are viciously and perversely attacked by mountaineers, their canoe trip explodes into horror and murder. Men stalk and are stalked along the river, and only the skilled and fittest will survive. The narrator becomes the leader and the man who must call on all his resources for survival.

The author, who became a celebrity poet in the 1960s was an avid woodsman, archer, and guitarist—all roles that play important parts in this novel. His profoundly masculine imagination and his mastery of putting his own myths in place, as well as his fascination with the English language, are reflected in the novel.

The river is the focal point and remains when all else dies or is forgotten. The book is dramatic in its vivid descriptions putting his reader directly into the action. Hollywood gave us Burt Reynolds as the star of the movie, but the river and Ed Gentry remain the stars of this descriptively written adventure story.

Ragtime
E. L. Doctorow (1931–)
New York: Random House, 1975

Mixing famous and infamous historical personages with fictional characters creates a clear view of the early twentieth century (1902-1917) in the U.S. The three families exemplify all walks of life and each person has his or her distinctive life, crossing paths at some point. The memorable figures of the documentary are Harry Houdini, the escape artist; Evelyn Nesbitt of the Shaw-White love triangle and murders; Commodore Perry at the North Pole; Henry Ford; J. P. Morgan, the capitalist; and socialist Emma Goldman preaching revolution and free love.

The fictional characters: a Lower East Side Jewish peddler and his daughter; the upper-middle-class family of Mother, Father, Mother's Younger Brother, Grandmother, and Young Son or Boy, all against the background of Scott Joplin's rags. Enter Coalhouse Walker, Jr., a Negro who does not know his place, and the world explodes as fact and fiction mingle. Being dragged to its destiny in World War I, the United States loses its innocence and gives birth to an age when anything and everything goes. A highly original concept and interesting and absorbing to read! In the late 1990s it became a hit Broadway musical.

Nickel Mountain
John Gardner (1933–1982)
New York: Knopf, 1973

Fat and forty with an uncertain future, gentle Henry Soames runs the Stop-Off Diner in the Catskills and contemplates the emptiness of his life. Enter Callie, a seventeen-year-old, plain neighbor who comes to work with him. Life changes when Henry marries her after she has become pregnant by a rich, local boy. This is a quiet novel of simplicity and warmth as small-town people try to live and understand the lives God has granted them, addressing moral dilemmas and human values. Darkness intrudes into the diner in the form of dangerous people and the sound of Henry's bad heart ticking, but it is overcome by Henry's understanding of himself, his love, his acceptance of life and death, and the support he receives from others.

Nickel Mountain is a folktale, a love story, and a religious tale. The characters, both sympathetic and weird, are memorable and, in their own ways, speak to modern society.

The World According to Garp
John Irving (1942–)
New York: Dutton, 1978

This fourth novel by John Irving established his critical reputation and commercial success. It is the wild and humorous, though tragic, story of the novelist T. S. Garp. Jenny Fields drops out of Wellesley to nurse war-shattered soldiers in a Boston hospital. She decides to have a child and gives herself to a dying soldier. In time her son, Garp, goes to a New England preparatory school where his mother, who wrote the book *A Sexual Suspect*, a statement on women's rights and sensibilities, serves as a nurse.

Jenny then goes on to become a leader in the women's rights movement. Garp also becomes a novelist and marries a bookish woman. The book contains bizarre characters in an exaggerated world. Most of the major characters are killed in a series of accidents. But the ideas of Garp and his mother about women and sensitive people continue to attract followers.

Being There
Jerzy N. Kosinski (1933–1991)
New York: Harcourt Brace Jovanovich, 1971

A parable for our times. An orphan, born by chance and so named Chance, is taken in by the Old Man. He is given a room with a bath, good food delivered to his door, and a choice of the Old Man's expensive castoff clothing. In exchange, he becomes the gardener—an illiterate young hermit, who is never to leave his garden. Consequently he becomes addicted to first radio and then television, which contain his only certain knowledge about his contemporary world.

When the Old Man dies, Chance is a nonperson without the paper identification demanded of our times, and he is cast out of the sheltered garden to the outside world. He becomes the famous savant Mr. Chauncey Gardiner, recognized for his brilliant, simplified observations about the state of the world, couched in terms of the growth and death of a garden. His reticence and desire for privacy are interpreted as wisdom and intelligence. Chance is the quintessential antihero and perhaps the man of the future. This is a story of suspense, humor, and irony, worth reading for its narrative and its truths about a complicated modern civilization seeking easy answers.

The Milagro Beanfield War
John Treadwell Nichols (1940–)
New York: Holt, Rinehart and Winston, 1974

Evidently it takes someone who has lived in or understands the culture of the American West to appreciate the laugh-out-loud humor of *Milagro*. One eastern critic called the characters stereotypes. They include an octogenarian who annually calls his family to a last visit only to continually outlive his descendants. Then there's an old lady who stands in her front yard on the plaza and throws rocks at certain passersbys, and a sheriff who always puts his boots on the wrong feet. We meet the driver of the pickup truck who daily parks at the town's only parking meter, forcing the law to write him a ticket, and a New York City VISTA worker horrified at the rawness of life. There is a Jewish lawyer who sides with the "peasants," and finally Joe Mondragon, who illegally diverts water from the irrigation ditch to raise a crop of beans on his ancestral lands. These humorous characters are to be laughed at and ignored as the white developers steal their water to provide for hotels, golf courses, and other recreational facilities.

When Joe waters his beans, for the first time the Hispanics in the valley fight back in their own inimitable way. As the conflict escalates, tragedy is scarcely avoided. This is Nichols's first book of a trilogy, documenting the Hispanic/Anglo war over that precious commodity in arid New Mexico: water. *Milagro* is effective with its humor as it addresses social justice and the American class system. Nichols spins wonderful tales with his compassion for people, his well-honed wit and his eye for vividly incongruous detail. But it seems to take a western reader to laugh.

The Bell Jar
Sylvia Plath (1932–1963)
New York: Harper & Row, 1971

A heartbreaking autobiographical novel that encompasses six months in the life of a young, talented woman who is beginning her chosen literary career, but whose life is being destroyed by her inability to cope. The story ends when she emerges from a mental hospital after a breakdown.

Sylvia Plath never resolved her own problems, as the character Esther Greenwood can never resolve hers. The novel depicts a liberated view of the modern American woman of her time, and the horrors of treatment of the mentally ill in the 1960s. Plath/Greenwood appears to be a victim of failures created by her historical era. Knowing that Plath will succeed as a suicide by the age of thirty taints the reading of the book. Although the author was creating a body of praised and sensitive poetry, her autobiographical figure is obsessed with death. Plath's premature death and this obsession often overwhelm the well-written novel and her volumes of poetry. The novel can be read as a social chronicle of coming of age in a particular time, but this story of a gifted young woman, out of contact with her world, feeling lonely and fragile and living in a bell jar sealing her off from everyone could be set in any era.

In 1998, Ted Hughes, Sylvia's estranged husband, who is often depicted as the villain in Plath's death because he left her for another woman, presented his side in his book of poetry, *Birthday Letters*. Reflecting the sustained interest in Plath and her work, Hughes's book is a bestseller, highly unusual for poetry. Hughes died of cancer shortly after his book's publication.

Even Cowgirls Get the Blues
Tom Robbins (1936–)
Boston: Houghton Mifflin, 1976

At birth, Sissy Hankshaw seems like just any other baby save for her large thumbs. Her working- class family in Richmond, Virginia, seems to accept this phenomena but draws the line when she starts hitchhiking around the countryside, frequently getting arrested.

Sissy grows up to become a very beautiful woman. But when the family decides to place her in a carnival, she runs away from home. This time she ends up in New York where she becomes acquainted with a man named The Countess. He introduces her to many famous people and she begins a modeling career. It is brought to the public's attention that her hands are never shown in any photographed shot, which becomes one of the mysteries of her popularity.

Sissy craves excitement, so the Countess ships her off to the Rubber Rose Ranch in the Dakotas, a wild health ranch for cowgirls. At the end, Sissy has surgery on her thumbs. From the beginning of the book, this seems to be an obvious solution to her physical handicap. But the results are very surprising. A wild and funny book by a popular writer.

The Killer Angels
Michael Shaara (1924–1988)
New York: McKay, 1974

War is hell! Especially brother against brother in the Civil War. But even on the same side a commanding brother must order his troops even if it means sending his lower ranking brother into the jaws of death. Although the book is fiction, most of the characters and events are true. And you are there—in the horror, the death defying attacks, the noise and smell of the ambushes, the slaughter of human beings, and the toll it takes on commanding officers, both on the winning and losing sides.

This is the bitterly fought battle of Gettysburg, seen day by bloody day from Monday, June 29, 1863, to Friday, July 3, 1863, and told by the men who were there making up two armies fighting for freedom and a way of life. It is not abstract but reality and the historical icons of war—

General Robert E. Lee, George Pickett, J. E. B. Stuart, Joshua Lawrence Chamberlain, George Gordon Meade, and Winfield Scott Hancock—are convincingly human.

Although many books have been written about this battle, here it is narrated as expertly as if the author had been a participant. He reveals men in the context of the times, men in action and men in thought within the shifts of battle. Here is the insight into what the war was about and what it meant. Reading the book is a draining emotional experience. Shed a tear for them and for yourself. The book won the Pulitzer Prize and was the basis of the movie *Gettysburg.*

Angle of Repose
Wallace Earle Stegner (1909–1993)
Garden City: Doubleday, 1971

Using author and illustrator Mary Halleck Foote's original letters, diaries and tales, Stegner has crafted a fictional four-generation novel which won the Pulitzer Prize in 1972.

Lyman Ward, critically ill and physically handicapped but mentally alert, resettles in his home and passes his time by writing a biography of his peripatetic western pioneering grandmother, Susan Burling Ward. Susan, raised in a genteel northeastern family and encouraged to develop her artistic talent, marries a stoic westerner, a mining engineer by trade. She follows him to California, Colorado, and Idaho as Oliver Ward dreams of projects that would civilize the West but do not bring him success.

Susan, feeling exiled and culturally impoverished, makes a home out of primitive conditions and often supports the family with her illustrated articles about her life. As seen through Lyman's eyes, the story shifts from past to present, with his grandfather's ineffectual dreams reflecting his own and his former wife's adulteries. This helps him to understand Susan and the difficulties between his childhood with Victorian parents, and the similar problems with his own children.

Through difficult times and often unresolved circumstances, past and present, the memorable characters reach an angle of repose, a geological term that denotes the angle at which dirt and pebbles stop rolling, a point of equilibrium. Stegner presents a noncliched view of the West—no gunfights, bad men, or threatening Indians, but instead the peopling of the area with its dramas, sorrows, and small happinesses that continue in the winning of the West.

Burr: A Novel
Gore Vidal (1925–)
New York: Random House, 1973

Were true history written so well, students would be clamoring to study the past. The vivid human characterizations of the founding fathers as seen through the eyes of the fictional Burr and his scribe, Charlie Schuyler, make American politics and government, with its intrigues, an exciting adventure story. Against the background of the presidential election in the 1830s, Burr at first reluctantly shares his anecdotes of the past when Jefferson, Hamilton, and Washington were not yet immortals but living beings with hopes and dreams, scrambling to succeed, failing and regrouping.

The presentation is the usual Gore Vidal—witty, acerbic, acidic, gossipy with his own modern political perspective clearly shown. Like his other historical novels, this one has a firm basis in reality. In his afterward he explains that he writes the historical novel to attribute motive to his characters. He tries to keep the known facts and whenever possible uses the actual phrases of the speaker.

With so much history to be learned through the historical novel, how great to have a superb writer giving a reasonable portrayal of our early years, if somewhat skewed through the eyes of Aaron Burr. It is guaranteed that one will never view the founding fathers in the same way again.

Fields of Fire

James H. Webb, Jr. (1946–)
Englewood Cliffs: Prentice Hall, 1978

A war like no other war ever fought by the United States is graphically and somewhat poignantly described by one who was there. The marine grunts on the nonexistent front lines (the fields of fire), which is so distinct from the officers at the rear. Racial tensions, misery, indiscriminate deaths of civilians, the horrors of the terrain, death by friendly fire, the hatred of the Vietnamese for the Americans, and the utter despair and futility of it all are scrutinized.

This is the game of war fought by men who signed up for repeated tours of duty in the hellhole that was Vietnam. Each man takes on a new identity as he joins the marines, speaks a new language understood only by insiders, and receives a new name often expressive of his performance. Thanks to Webb's skill, the reader knows these men well: why they are there, why they act and think as they do, and how the few are hated and unable to adjust on their return home.

For one who lived through these times Stateside, the escalating protests against the war and the nightly body counts on television come vividly to mind. *Fields* tells the powerful story of a platoon of tough, young marines fighting in Vietnam. It expresses man's basic ambiguity about war, its dangers and destruction, contrasted with its attraction as man's ultimate game and his ability to survive. These are boys from the ghettos, small towns, and farms in America, who are involved in a war no one understands. Vietnam becomes the only reality and war is the game these men play best. As stated by critics, this is the best battlefield novel of Vietnam. Regardless of one's stand at the time or in retrospect, read it at your peril. It will challenge your thinking.

The 1980s
The Age of Communications

The first Space Shuttle is launched.

The first genetic engineering product (Insulin) reaches the market.

Unemployment exceeds 10% for the first time since the Depression.

The computer dramatically changes the way people live and do business.

The World Series is postponed when an earthquake rocks Candlestick Park in San Francisco.

The AT&T telephone monopoly is broken into local "Baby Bells."

MTV, the first all-music network, begins serving cable subscribers.

Sandra Day O'Connor becomes the first woman to sit on the Supreme Court.

The compact disc, or CD, is developed and by 1991 will outsell music vinyl records and tapes.

Federal researchers isolate the virus thought to cause Acquired Immune Deficiency Syndrome (AIDS).

Stock market plunges 508 points in a single day surpassing Black Tuesday in 1929.

The supertanker *Exxon Valdez* runs aground off the coast of Alaska, causing the worst oil spill in U.S. history.

The Hunt for Red October
Tom Clancy (1947–)
Annapolis: Naval Institute Press, 1984

As Cold War tensions heighten in the mid-1980s, a Soviet nuclear submarine captain makes a valiant effort to defect to the United States, taking with him *Red October*, a top-secret Soviet vessel. Both the Soviet navy, who recognize the defector in their midst, and the U.S. Navy, who fear that *Red October* is positioning itself for an attack on the Eastern seaboard, attempt to block the captain's efforts in a thrilling game of cat-and-mouse. While tensions heighten, U.S. Naval Academy instructor Jack Ryan saves the day, using a combination of action-hero bravery and coolheaded acumen. Published by the Naval Institute Press, *The Hunt for Red October* introduced the world to future blockbuster author Tom Clancy.

While Clancy's first novel did not break ground in its basic premise as a military espionage thriller, its novelty instead lay in the richly detailed technical descriptions that he provided of both Soviet and U.S. military hardware. So realistic were Clancy's descriptions that he was allegedly debriefed by the government as to the source of his information. In its descriptions of American military might and waning Soviet power, Clancy's novel provided the ideal vision of America in the Reagan years, a vision also reflected in Jack Ryan, who will rise through the ranks of the U.S. government in sequels, eventually becoming president.

Ironweed
William Kennedy (1928–)
New York: Viking, 1983

It's All Hallow's Eve in 1938 and a bum—an unusual bum—Francis Phelan, contacts the dead in their graves and sees apparitions as he moves around his old home in Albany, New York. As he works as a gravedigger, he listens and speaks back to "his likable father, his hateful mother, and his thirteen-day-old son."

Francis sleeps in flophouses and eats at the mission. He hasn't seen his family in twenty-two years. He has gone on to be a murderer. Moving through the city's underside with his equally down-and-out companion, Helen, Francis revisits all the occasions of his guilt and can now think of plausible alibis and excuses for his actions, which have led him to this seamy life of violence and poverty. He still seeks something he can value and this takes him back to the past and a visit with his family.

This is the third in a series of Albany novels and is generally considered Kennedy's best. The book's presentation is essentially a comic one, with no sentimentality and with a freshness of language and originality of black humor.

Lonesome Dove

Larry McMurty (1936–)
New York: Simon & Schuster, 1985

A novel of epic proportions covering a period of American history after the Civil War, the book opens in Texas where a group of cowboys are mired down in a boring existence. Life consists of feeding cattle, breaking in horses, and going into the town of Lonesome Dove to drink and give the local whores "a poke." Of course there are barroom fights for any slight, but the men have to rid themselves of so much energy. Card playing is a recreation that can go on for days, and many of the men seem to have no purpose in life but just to drift. Eventually the leaders of the group decide to round up a huge herd of cattle and horses and make their fortune by a 2,000-mile drive to Montana. They are not above trekking into Mexico to steal additional livestock and better-riding horses but somehow manage to return to Texas unscathed.

Although there are numerous personal subplots, the main theme of this book is the treacherous cattle drive these men make. If they can trek twenty miles in one day, it is considered successful. They are threatened by numerous Indian attacks, rainstorms, and lightning strikes, which not only kill animals but riders as well. Dust storms and locust scourges are common, and heavy rain can build up a stream or river to the point that it is impassable for days at a time.

Yet, as difficult as it is dealing with the elements, feuds between the cowboys can be more deadly. Most of the life-hardened men are incapable of feeling any sensitivity for others. There are respites from the perils of the cattle drive and tales of a more romantic nature. One cowboy brings a whore, Lorena, along on the journey and then leaves her alone while he goes into town to gamble. When she is kidnapped by an Indian outlaw and taken to another territory, it's one of his sidekicks who rescues Lorena. Another *Lonesome Dove* character is searching for the wife who has left him for an old boyfriend. And there's a man who hankers for a woman who left him seventeen years before to marry someone else. We also meet the female rancher who manages to keep the old homestead, despite the fact that her husband was kicked in the head by a horse and becomes comatose. It is a very tough life on the trail.

Beloved
Toni Morrison (1931–)
New York: Knopf, 1987

A strange and distressing story, but outlining the plot does not explain the emotional impact on the reader. Sethe is proud and beautiful. Escaped from slavery, she is haunted by her heritage, as are those around her. She loves her daughter so fiercely that she kills her rather than allowing her to be taken back into bondage. Living in rural Ohio several years after the Civil War, Sethe must cope with this hunted life on every level, challenging her body and her spirit.

Honored many times for *Beloved*, including the Pulitzer Prize in 1988 and the prestigious Nobel Prize in Literature in 1993, Morrison has written a haunting tale made more horrifying by the beauty and lyrical quality of its telling. She captures the vernacular with all the layers of English heard in African-American speech. She explores the psyche and the enduring spirit of the people, and the characters come alive. She gives us a way to see what we have not seen, both the strange and the familiar, and alters our perceptions of the black experience. She is the master of evocative language.

And Ladies of the Club
Helen Hooven Santmyer (1895–1986)
Columbus: Ohio State University Press, 1982

The naming of this book as a Book-of-the-Month-Club selection was front-page news. The author who wrote it over a fifty year period, was then eighty eight years old and living in a nursing home. For obvious human-interest reasons, Helen Santmyer was a media dream. Her story is a novel true to a middle America, small-town way of life.

In 1888 in Waynesboro, Ohio, on graduation day at Waynesboro Female College, Anne and Sally Cochran are asked to join some faculty wives, teachers, and a few local grande dames in organizing a women's club of twelve who will meet to read and discuss papers dealing with literary subjects. The book ends in 1932 with the death of Anne, the last of the founding members.

With the club serving as a framework, the citizens and their town are revealed. Anne marries a doctor and Sally marries a Union Army veteran who successfully revitalizes the town's failing rope and twine factory. The town's history is seen through the eyes of the original club members and then through the eyes of their children, grandchildren, and great grand-children.

The ladies gossip, carefully select their membership, do good works such as establishing a public library, and all too often mourn the deaths of their children. A trolley line and new hospital are built, and then local industries begin to emerge. There are weddings, funerals, celebrations, tragic fires, and epidemics. The economy rises and falls and the boys fight in the Great War in France. Each chapter begins with the membership of the club, new sur-names appear, names drop to an "In Memoriam" column and new names are added—the natural rhythm of generations. One woman wishes to write a rebuttal to Sinclair Lewis's depiction of the Midwest, and if this is the book, unlike Lewis's, it is neither sentimental nor satiric. There are different women of the club but all, with their surroundings, are interesting.

The Joy Luck Club
Amy Tan (1952–)
New York: Putnam, 1989

Rarely has the long-standing, historical conflict between mothers and daughters been so wondrously told. The traditional clash of two genera-tions is heightened by the difference in cultures—raised in China with the United States as the adopted home or country.

But it is more than generational. The energy comes from the tension between two worlds: the old country world of China with its arranged marriages and the subjugation of women; backcountry villages; mystical beliefs; tyranny of family; rumbling poverty; classed society; and the new world of the United States: malls, suburbs, and a vague angst in the midst of middle-class comfort.

Amy Tan is a wonderful writer, a master at dialogue and description. *The Joy Luck Club* is especially appealing to and widely read by high school and college women as they seek to understand their relationships with their own mothers, regardless of culture.

A Confederacy of Dunces
John Kennedy Toole (1937–1969)
Baton Rouge: Louisiana State University Press, 1980

Ignatius J. Reilly is one of the weirdest characters you will ever meet in American fiction. He is neither likable nor lovable, but he is both an interesting and a funny lunatic when you are not totally disgusted with him. He is surrounded by equally unusual people, "a confederacy of dunces," who can at times make the ridiculous Ignatius look almost normal.

In the novel set in New Orleans, the characters leave their mark and are shaped by the city. The numerous characters include the mother, Mrs. Reilly; her matchmaking friend Santa Battaglia; Miss Trixie, the octogenarian and assistant accountant at Levy Pants; the Levys; the inept patrolman Mancuso; and Jones, the jivecat in dark glasses. The slob Ignatius is in revolt against the entire modern age, lying in bed filling Big Chief tablets with invective. This, coupled with his inability to get and hold a decent job, propels the ludicrous actions. Each job is a disaster but with a certain logic of its own. The love story with his girlfriend, Myrna Minkoff of the Bronx, is like no other boy–girl relationship ever told.

But it all comes back to Ignatius—pseudo intellectual, deadbeat, goof-off, braggart, and glutton who repels others—a son even a mother finds hard to love. The reader is compelled to laugh but the book is more than comedy; it is farcical and also tragic. Ignatius and other characters conjure up pity in the reader. Enjoy a trip to an exotic city with its unique vernacular and customs captured in its back streets, old neighborhoods, homosexuals, lower-class whites, and a sympathetically but realistically portrayed black. Go visit Ignatius memorialized in bronze loitering in perpetuity outside the former D. H. Holmes Department Store. And while reading, laugh out loud.

John Kennedy Toole died before his only novel was published. The book won the Pulitzer Prize in 1981.

The Accidental Tourist
Anne Tyler (1941–)
New York: Knopf, 1985

This is a story of the war between our desires for safety and for adventure. Macon Leary, a travel writer who hates both travel and change or surprise, is threatened by divorce and a drastic change in lifestyle when his wife leaves him. He adjusts by creating absurd efficiencies, but he can't control his dog, Edward. A dog obedience course brings trainer Muriel Pritchett, with her extreme dress and hairstyle, into Macon's life. She appears to be an unlikely companion for him.

After breaking his leg, Macon must move into the home of his dysfunctional Leary family. However, it's a toss-up as to which household in its distinctive way is the most crazily disorganized—the Learys or the Pritchetts? The plot centers on whether Macon will return to his steady wife Sarah or risk aligning with Muriel. The reader cheers first for one, then the other, while laughing at the comic yet compassionate scenes.

The Color Purple
Alice Walker (1944–)
New York: Harcourt Brace Jovanovich, 1982

Several generations out of slavery and the southern Negro is not faring well. Black and white lines are still clearly drawn. Many black families are dysfunctional, and the men in their frustration try to subjugate their women and often abuse them. Babies, wanted and unwanted, proliferate.

Celie learns to survive, writing poignant letters to God in Negro pathos, not expecting divine intervention, but God is the only one who will listen and not tell her secrets. Her life is hard before her husband's mistress, Shug Avery, a flamboyant blues singer, appears and teaches Celie how to laugh and love. Celie's beloved sister Nettie leads a different life as an educated missionary to the Olinkas in Africa. Her letters to her sister speak of trials, as a road built by white men destroys the village, the natives' culture and lives, all in the cause of progress.

Told in a melodic southern dialect, this is a story of intense emotion, memorable characters, revealing whole worlds not readily known of blacks and whites, of God and love, of men and women, and nature in its glory.

The Bonfire of the Vanities
Tom Wolfe (1931–)
New York: Farrar Straus, 1987

Sherman McCoy has it all, or at least all in a shallow, superficial world. Sherm is a successful bond salesman in one of Wall Street's prodigious firms, making close to a million dollars a year. His beautiful, Upper East Side penthouse has been lavishly embellished by his interior-decorator wife, Judy, and together they have produced a lovely daughter who binds them together. The marriage is fragile but in a society that focuses on wealth rather than humanity this does not seem to be a serious concern. Meanwhile, Sherman has taken a mistress, Maria, who is married to a much older multimillionaire. Their liaisons are arranged in a sublet, rent-controlled apartment, that is used only for their illicit affairs. Sherman and Maria seem made for each other.

Life is wonderful until the two of them are involved in a hit-and-run accident in which a black man is seriously injured. They agree not to report the mishap. For several days Sherman reads *The City Light*, a New York tabloid, to see if any mention is made of the calamity. With the passage of time he feels confident that the incident was too insignificant to make the news. But then a radical black leader, the Reverend Reggie Bacon, and Peter Fallow, a British journalist on the *City Light* staff, try to find the guilty party. Sherman is the first defendant tracked down by the media's investigators, and he is brought to court and jailed briefly before his bond is posted. Maria safely escapes the legal system as she flies to Italy in the arms of a new lover.

This is a very disturbing look at racial issues in our society today. The Reverend Bacon is depicted as a hate-filled rabble-rouser. Even the assistant district attorney loses his perspective and is caught up in the pandemonium, realizing that the case can make him a star. Does justice triumph in this case? You will have to be the judge.

The 1990s
Preparing for the Millennium

The United States launches Operation Desert Storm in Iraq.

The Americans with Disabilities Act is passed.

Floods ravage the Midwest.

The North American Free Trade Agreement is approved by Congress.

The Oklahoma City Bombing kills 168 people.

McDonald's, the fast food chain, opens to acclaim and long lines in Moscow.

Jubilant Germans tear down the Berlin Wall, allowing free travel between East and West Berlin.

The information superhighway links sources of information worldwide.

The House of Representatives impeaches President William Clinton, who is acquitted in the Senate.

Garry Kasparov, one of the best chess players ever, is defeated by an IBM computer called *Deep Blue*.

Titanic becomes the top-grossing film of all time.

High-tech companies watch stock prices greatly increase and then crash.

The Alienist
Caleb Carr (1955–)
New York: Random House, 1994

Dr. Laszlo Kreizler, an alien abnormal psychologist with an unusual ability to solve crimes, works against the rich background of 1890s New York City with its underworld and its contrasting opulence.

It is a dark, brooding story as the group recruited by New York's reform police commissioner, Teddy Roosevelt, searches for a serial killer who is slaughtering boy prostitutes. At every turn crime bosses thwart the investigators and the city's hidden rulers, especially J. Pierpont Morgan.

With its mixture of fictional characters and historical personages playing major roles in an authentic New York, the story has a strong nonfiction, historical feel. The author explores the evil side of the human psyche and reveals the terrors and tragedies that cause men to kill. The mystery is well plotted and suspenseful while the odd collection of characters observe, discover, and capture the murderer.

The late nineteenth century is a fascinating backdrop for an intelligent, humorous, and terrifying detective story with an ambiance set for gruesome murders and scary searches through dark streets. An imaginative book that is entertaining and engrossing despite its grisly content. Its sequel *The Angel of Darkness* (1997) with a horrifying female villain who is almost equal in wits to the detective team, is a satisfying continuation of New York's bleak scene with the excitement and adventure of *The Alienist*.

Underworld
Don DeLillo (1936–)
New York: Scribners, 1997

This is the story of a baseball that Ralph Branca of the Dodgers pitched in the 1951 playoff game and Bobby Thomson of the Giants hit for a game-winning home run—"the shot heard round the world." Well, sort of. It's the story of the explosion of a sonic nuclear test, a second shot heard round the world on the same day. It is also the biography of Nick Shay's transition from juvenile delinquent to esteemed waste analyst—in a way. But it depicts the United States in the last half of the twentieth century in bits and pieces, the Cold War backward from the 1990s to the 1950s and forward again. It explores how people rearranged their lives in order to live with mutual assured destruction with its terror and absurdity.

Underworld is a magnificent, sprawling, epochal, common history that reveals the essence of underworld America from the Bronx to Phoenix, and it defies a summation of story line. The prologue is an exciting piece that captures the emotions of the playoff baseball game, and the ball reappears throughout the rest of the novel, finally residing with Nick Shay at a cost of $34,500. Nick explains that the ball signifies not Thomson's winning home run but Branca's losing pitch.

Regardless of the disparate parts, everything is linked. Somehow everything also connects, such as the Cuban Missile Crisis, Lenny Bruce and his monologues, classical music and jazz, the atom bomb, garbage recycling, a baseball, Jayne Mansfield, the recurrence of the number 13, Truman Capote's Black and White Ball, J. Edgar Hoover, Sister Edgar, fictional characters, Nick's younger brother Matt, Bronx housewife Klara Sax who becomes a famous artist. A revealing, exciting tale.

Cold Mountain
Charles Frazier (1950–)
New York: Atlantic Monthly Press, 1997

Cold Mountain unexpectedly exploded as popular fiction in 1997. It relates the story of two journeys and their travails. The wounded Confederate soldier Inman walks away from the ravages of war and seeks his way home to the Blue Ridge and his sweetheart. Intelligence, crafty moves, necessary violence, and his determination to reach Cold Mountain and a thread of hope overcome his severe trials and tribulations. He is Everyman walking the rough road of life.

The young woman he left behind, Ada, struggles to survive on the farm after her father's death. With the help of the pragmatic drifter Ruby, Ada's life changes beyond recognition during the war years and she becomes one with the rugged Blue Ridge Mountains rather than her native Charleston. Not truly a book of the Civil War (although battle scenes are recollected and described in detail), not truly a love story (although Inman is seeking Ada), it refutes classification as any one genre. Using selected true stories passed down by the author's great-great-grandfather, Frazier develops the life of Inman with vivid writing, careful research of nineteenth-century mountain life and believable dialogue, producing a gripping first novel.

Snow Falling on Cedars
David Gusterson (1956–)
New York: Harcourt Brace, 1994

Here we have a classic whodunit with serious racial undertones. Set on the coast of Washington State in the mid-1950s, Kabuo Miyamoto stands accused of murdering fisherman Carl Heine, Jr. As the courtroom drama unfolds, many anecdotes about the lives of Kabuo, Carl, and the newspaper reporter, Ishmael Chambers, evolve. All the men have survived World War II, returning home with hopes of resuming a normal life. For Ishmael this would not be an easy task since he had suffered permanent wounds in battle, including the loss of one arm. He never marries because of this injury, and also because he has always loved Kabuo's wife, Hatsu. Their brief romance was doomed from the start since Japanese parents were so unrelenting that children never marry outside their race. Yet Ishmael cannot forget the woman he loved so deeply.

Prior to the war, it was illegal for aliens to own land in the United States. This was particularly distressing for Kabuo's father Zenhichi, who has always worked for American farmers in the strawberry fields. When a plot of seven acres of land becomes available, he arranges a lease-to-own agreement with Carl Heine, Sr. The terms are a $500 down payment and subsequent payments of $256 to be paid semiannually for eight years. During the war the Miyamotos are sent to the internment camps and the final payments are impossible to make. Carl Sr. then sells the land to another neighbor. It is a source of extreme bitterness to the Miyamotos that they were betrayed when a balance of only $512 remained unpaid and this may be a motive for the son's murder. Ishmael gains access to some evidence that will prove that Kabuo might not be the murderer. But he also realizes that a guilty verdict would send him to prison and Hatsu in her loneliness could turn to Ishmael. Snow falls heavily on cedars throughout the trial. The outcome is spellbinding and there are many twists to this story.

Pigs in Heaven
Barbara Kingsolver (1955–)
New York: Harper Collins, 1993

The biblical wisdom of King Solomon, who decreed to split the baby between two claimants, causing a satisfactory resolution, is given a modern twist.

Taylor, a single Anglo woman of limited means, takes in, loves, and is successfully raising an abandoned Indian baby under difficult circumstances. As a six year old, Turtle witnesses a freak accident at Hoover Dam, convinces her mother of what she has seen, and a man is dramatically rescued. Her action and the media attention that follow draw the notice of the Cherokee Nation and the conflict begins over who should appropriately raise Turtle: the mother who loves her or the people of her culture. The crisis compels the flight of Turtle and Taylor, disrupting the lives of all around them.

This is a beautifully told story of heartbreak and redeeming love that tests the boundaries of family and culture. An enchanting story set in the urban southwest and the Cherokee Nation in Oklahoma holds the reader with a fast-moving plot and characters whom you want to find resolution and happiness.

Although the book stands on its own, it is essentially a sequel to *The Bean Trees* in which Taylor and Turtle are first introduced. Reading one book by Barbara Kingsolver, who is an eloquent, poignant, and witty master storyteller who throws a liberal dose of miracles in her plot makes the reader want to seek out more. A writer of and about the present who should survive the critics of time.

The Shipping News
E. Annie Proulx (1935–)
New York: Scribners, 1993

An unusual tale with somewhat unattractive characters whom you grow to like. Quoyle, a third-rate newspaper hack, described as having "a head like a crenshaw, no neck, reddish hair," is faced with wrenching change as he gets his two emotionally disturbed daughters from his two-timing wife, who is subsequently killed in an automobile accident. An aunt persuades him to move with her to the starkly beautiful coastal landscape of their ancestral home in Newfoundland.

On desolate Quoyle's Point in a house abandoned over forty years, they begin new lives but still must cope with a future, the immediate past, as well as the unsavory acts of ancestors. This is an isolated place of cruel storms, a ruined fishing industry, and chronic unemployment, a country where the temperature rarely goes above 70 degrees and travel is easier by boat or snowmobile. The aunt becomes a yacht upholsterer and Quoyle reports the shipping news for the local weekly, *Gammy Bird*, which specializes in sexual abuse stories and grisly photos of car accidents. Especially during the first winter the Quoyles must face their demons, overcome catastrophes, and have some minor triumphs as they become part of the community with its myriad characters, each of whom has adapted in his or her own way to this harsh life and their own woes.

Each chapter is named for a knot, described and illustrated that exemplifies the happenings. Both comic and dark, this is great storytelling with satisfying and appropriate dialogue. It is different and leaves you fulfilled. A Pulitzer Prize winner.

The Stone Diaries
Carol Shields (1935–)
New York: Viking, 1994

A triple hit! A Pulitzer Prize winner (among other awards), a *New York Times* best-seller and a book that is actually read, enjoyed, discussed, and recommended to others. *Stone Diaries* is an engrossing fictional autobiography of a woman's life that encompasses the twentieth century. Like all memory, it is selective.

Daisy is a witness to her own life, birth, and death. She often wonders who she is, and what she is to become—a woman in search of herself. Events in her life are also seen through the eyes of her children, her friends and relations, letters, newspaper columns, and mementos. Her poignant story is superbly written and cannot be assigned to any genre—it is in a class by itself. Daisy is not an out-of-the-ordinary woman, but one whose life absorbs the reader into really caring about her.

A Thousand Acres
Jane Smiley (1949–)
New York: Knopf, 1991

A rather simple, basic story of a family and its farm gradually escalates into horror, death, as well as mental and emotional disintegration. Shakespeare's *King Lear* in Iowa. Because the book is so well written, the reader is lulled into a sense of complacency where nothing much happens, continues while the plot gradually explodes into a dysfunctional family, skewed relationships, incest, suicide, and the disintegration of marriages. The surface does not reveal the secrets hidden below.

Larry Cook, respected aging patriarch of a rich thriving farm, suddenly prepares to decree his land to his three daughters: Ginny and Rose and their husbands who live and work on the farm, and Caroline, a Des Moines lawyer who rejects the idea. The ensuing family conflict spills into the community as neighbors and friends take sides with Father, the long-suffering daughters on the farm, or Caroline and her legal actions. The novel begins to haunt the reader as the individuals reveal their ruthless, divided natures, and the reader must rethink his or her opinion of the characters.

An extraordinary novel of insight and interaction of humans and events in which are raised profound questions about conduct, moral responsibility, and family relationships—all set against a background of farming in America today. Although the relationship of farmer to land is vividly drawn and essential to events, the human actions are universal. Reading *A Thousand Acres* leaves one wanting more of Jane Smiley's talents. A Pulitzer Prize winner.

Three Popular Novels

Love Story
Erich Segal (1937–)
New York: Macmillan, 1970

Jonathan Livingston Seagull
Richard Bach (1936–)
New York: Macmillan, 1970

The Bridges of Madison County
Robert James Waller (1939–)
New York: Warner Books, 1992

Much to the chagrin of literary critics, some books will become best-sellers and will be read by "just everybody." The more the book is disparaged, the more it is read and elevated to cult status. Such is the fate of Waller's *Bridges*, Bach's *Jonathan Livingston Seagull* and Segal's *Love Story*.

In *Bridges* truth follows fiction. With the popularity of the book and the movie, even *National Geographic* acknowledges the fictional photographer Robert Kincaid. An unexpected, intense, emotional love affair happens between the peripatetic loner, who is the last cowboy, and a mid-forties Iowa farmwife, but responsibility to family wins over love. An old story retold that can still elicit tears in the reader and sobs in the moviegoer. Fortunately the book is short.

In *Seagull* Jonathan aspires to fly as no seagull has before, and his accomplishments are disparaged instead of praised by his peers. With divine intervention and the power of love, he rises to greater heights and trains young gulls to look beyond themselves. A morality story or the study of the aerodynamics of flight, with photographs.

To be a beautiful love story it must end in tragedy and redemption. Short and poignant *Love Story* pits the formula with the reconciliation of Oliver Barrett IV with his father, Oliver Barrett III. Presumably in the 1970s all bright, brilliant jocks at "Haavad" and all poor, brilliant, immigrant descendant Radcliffe women spoke in wiseacre repartee. (Old friend Erich Segal may have used Vice President Al Gore and wife Tipper as models for the uptight preppy and his free-spirited girlfriend.) Anyone today can quote the adage "Love means never having to say you're sorry." According to *Civilization* magazine even the author in 1999 was not too sure what it meant.

One positive aspect of these books: since they are so widely known, they provide grist for television satires. Takeoffs abound. Also, any book that gets large numbers of people to read can't be all bad.

Personal Life List: Twentieth Century Novels Read

(These Pages May Be Duplicated for Your Use)

	Read	Date	Comment
The Accidental Tourist			
Advise and Consent			
The Age of Innocence			
The Agony and the Ecstasy			
The Alienist			
All the King's Men			
An American Tragedy			
And Ladies of the Club			
Andersonville			
Angle of Repose			
Anthony Adverse			
Archie and Mehitabel			
Babbitt			
Being There			
A Bell for Adano			
The Bell Jar			
Beloved			
The Big Sky			
The Big Sleep			
The Blackboard Jungle			
The Bonfire of the Vanities			
Breakfast at Tiffany's			
The Bridge of San Luis Rey			
Burr: A Novel			
By Love Possessed			
The Caine Mutiny			
The Call of the Wild			
Catch-22			

	Read	**Date**	**Comment**

The Catcher in the Rye
The Chosen
The Circular Staircase
The Color Purple

A Confederacy of Dunces
The Confessions of Nat Turner
Cold Mountain
The Day of the Locust

Death Comes for the Archbishop
A Death in the Family
Deliverance
Delta Wedding

Drums Along the Mohawk
Early Autumn: A Story of a Lady
Even Cowgirls Get the Blues
Exodus

Fahrenheit 451
Fields of Fire
The Fixer
For Whom the Bell Tolls

The Fountainhead
From Here to Eternity
Gentleman's Agreement
A Girl of the Limberlost

The Godfather
Gone with the Wind
The Good Earth
Go Tell It on the Mountain

The Grapes of Wrath
The Great Gatsby
The Great Santini
The Group

	Read	Date	Comment

The Heart Is a Lonely Hunter
The Human Comedy
The Hunt for Red October
I Heard the Owl Call My Name

I Never Promised You a Rose Garden
Invisible Man
Ironweed
The Joy Luck Club

The Jungle
The Keys of the Kingdom
The Killer Angels
Kings Row

Kitty Foyle
The Last Hurrah
The Late George Apley
The Light in the Forest

Little Big Man
Lolita
Lonesome Dove
Look Homeward, Angel

Lost Horizon
The Magnificent Ambersons
The Maltese Falcon
The Man in the Gray Flannel Suit

The Man Who Killed the Deer
The Man with the Golden Arm
The Milagro Beanfield War
The Monkey Wrench Gang

Mountain Man
The Moviegoer
Mr. Blandings Builds His Dream House
The Naked and the Dead

	Read	Date	Comment

Native Son
Nickel Mountain
Northwest Passage
No Time for Sergeants

On the Road
One Flew over the Cuckoo's Nest
The Ox-Bow Incident
Peyton Place

Pigs in Heaven
Portnoy's Complaint
The Postman Always Rings Twice
Rabbit, Run

Ragtime
Raintree County
The Rector of Justin
Red Sky at Morning

Riders of the Purple Sage
The Robe
Seize the Day
A Separate Peace

Shane
Ship of Fools
The Shipping News
Shogun

Slaughterhouse-Five
Smoky, the Cowhorse
Snow Falling on Cedars
So Big

The Sound and the Fury
The Stone Diaries
Strange Fruit
Stranger in a Strange Land

	Read	Date	Comment

Studs Lonigan: A Trilogy
Tales of the South Pacific
Ten North Frederick
Them

This Side of Innocence
A Thousand Acres
Three Popular Novels
Tobacco Road

To Kill a Mockingbird
The Treasure of the Sierra Madre
A Tree Grows in Brooklyn
Tropic of Cancer

Trout Fishing in America
True Grit
Underworld
Up the Down Staircase

U.S.A. Trilogy
Vein of Iron
The Virginian
The Wapshot Chronicle

What Makes Sammy Run?
Winesburg, Ohio
The World According to Garp
The Yearling

You Know Me Al
The Young Lions

Your Other Selected Favorites

Read	Date	Comment